Vol.1 ISSUE #5

Published by Eastern Heroes Publishing
Produced by Rick Baker

Design & layout
Tim Hollingsworth
Instagram: 79_design

Printing: Ingramspark

Contributors:

UK
Rick Baker, Michael Nesbitt,
Johnny Burnett, Simon Pritchard,
Dean Meadows, Alan Donkin,
Ron Ivey, Aiodhan M Cochrane,
Shazad Asghar, Dave Cater,
Martin Sandison

USA
Jason McNeil, Hector Martinez,
Demetrius Angelo

GERMANY
Thorsten Boose

Special Thanks
Robert Samuels, Carl Scott,
Amy Johnston, Ron Van Clief,
Vincent Lyn

All rights reserved. No part of this publication may be reproduced or transmitted in any or by any means, graphic, electronic or mechanical, including photocopying, recording, taping or any information storage and retrieval system, without prior written permission of the publisher.
© 2021 Eastern Heroes.

Editorial

Here we are again, with another bumper packed edition. This issue we dedicate a section to promote the 10th anniversary of "The Urban Action Showcase" This is another bumper issue packed with many articles and interviews. The front cover depicts the celebrities at this years "Urban showcase" featuring interviews with, Amy Johnston, Roy Van Clief, Robert Samuels, and Vincent Lyn and Carl Scott. Also attending will be Don the Dragon Wilson, and Taimak sadly I ran out of time to interview both of these iconic actors, but I will be meeting both these guys at the "Urban Showcase" and will feature them in a future edition. Taimak Guarriello, known mononymously as Taimak, an American martial artist, actor, and stuntman known for his lead role as Leroy Green in the 1985 martial arts film 2The Last Dragon2, Taimak's leading role in which he played Leroy Green, a Bruce Lee-inspired martial artist in search of "The Glow," was his first major break in acting. The film was a financial success and grossed more than $25 million at the box office. which I saw at the cinema when it opened in 1985 and loved it. This has become a cult film amongst many over the years and it is a shame that he never followed up with a sequel but he did a number of TV roles and music videos including the lead male in Janet Jackson's "Let's Wait Awhile" music video and Debbie Allen's "Special Look" video. He played a date rapist in an episode of the TV show A Different World. He appeared in 36 Crazyfists' music video "Bloodwork." And then there is Don "the Dragon" Wilson. Donald Glen Wilson (born September 10, 1954), nicknamed "The Dragon", is an American martial artist, film actor, and former professional kick boxer.[1] An 11-time world champion who scored 47 knockouts in four decades, he has been called by the STAR System Ratings as "perhaps the greatest kick boxer in American history. He has disposed of more quality competition than anyone we've ever ranked" Don has had a movie career spanning from 1982 and is still currently making films today. Some of his best known films include "Bloodfist" "Ring of Fire" "the Martial Arts Kid" and "Death Fighter" to name a few. There are so many great features in this issue that as always it goes over the page count to cram it all in. I would like to thank all those that have taken part in interviews and contributed articles and a big thank you to Crike99Art for the great cover and Tim Hollingsworth for doing a sterling job putting this issue together, So until the next issue coming soon...

Keep the faith

Rick Baker

Contents

2. Yuen Biao: Golden Little Fortune
11. Enter The Black Dragon
19. Revengeance: Death Games
    & Angry Ranger
23. Kwan Tak-Hing
27. Jackie Chanimation
38. Ratings Kung Fusion
42. Jackie at Prince Charles Cinema
44. JUGANDO CON FUEGO
47. Spotlight: Aiodhan M Cochrane
50. Scarlett Cross
    Battle from script to screen
53. Bruce Lee Pilgrimage
56. Urban Action Showcase
66. Carl Scott Interview
71. UASE - Legacy & Lineage
73. Game Of Death Redux 2.0 review
75. Wireless Kung Fu
78. Alamo Drafthouse
82. Amy Johnston Interview
86. Vincent Lyn Interview
91. 5 fingers of discs

元彪 YUEN BIAO 元彪

Golden Little Fortune

By Martin Sandison

There's a sequence near the beginning of Sammo Hung's action comedy par excellence, Millionare's Express, wherein Yuen Baio is stuck on the top of a burning building. In a wide shot, he side flips four stories on to the ground, gets up, runs and delivers a line of dialogue. Yuen himself said there were only tatami mats to break his fall, and due to his training he avoided breaking his back. It's one of the all-time best stunts in Hong Kong cinema, and matches anything Jackie Chan ever did. Perhaps it will remain the frames of film that Yuen will be most remembered for. But that would be a damn shame. The man has graced countless classics, as a stuntman, actor, choreographer, and even doubled for Frankie Chan's outrageous kicks in Prodigal Son, a stuntman standing in for his own character! With this article I want to share my thoughts on two of Yuen's movies, one very well known and one less so, both very important in his canon.

One of the most rare Hong Kong movies ever made, License to Steal was given a Laserdisc release back in the day and made it on to VCD, but never DVD.

I managed to get my hands on a copy converted to DVD some years ago. What's so ironic about this movie is that in a simple stunt at the end of the film a stuntman lost his life, one of the only times in Hong Kong film history – and it's very hard to own the film! It's a shame, because this is classic early 90's fare, enlivened by superb fight scenes and that anything-goes energy. Despite having a supporting role, Yuen's is the most interesting character and gets the lions share of great action. Hung (Joyce Godenz), Hsiao Yen (Alvina Kong) and Ngan (Agnes Aurelio) are professional thieves whose lives are fraught with danger, but they love living on the edge. When Ngan goes against them and their master, leaving the other two for dead, so begins a deadly game of cat and mouse. Swordsman (Yuen Baio) pops up to help the duo and two cops (Richard Ng and Collin Chou) get involved as the plot descends in to OTT silliness. Interestingly, License to Steal is directed by Billy Chan Lung, whose brother Peter Chan has a cameo. The latter is known for his acting roles in classics such as Prodigal Son and Odd Couple, and was on the receiving end of Bruce Lee's first explosive kicks in The Big Boss. Billy Chan was also a veteran stuntman and assistant action director for such luminaries as Sammo Hung. He directs with a sure hand, and has a knack for characters introductory scenes: Both Yuen Baio and Richard Ng's are masterclasses of framing and atmosphere. The lighting and compositions are of a high standard

License to Steal (1990)

throughout the film, especially the action and burglary scenes. It's a bit odd that Billy Chan didn't really break through as a director for major productions, seeing as his ability is evident.

Yuen's character seems to be an extension of the one he played in , with not as much screen time. Swordsman is from Mainland China, which lends a bit of depth to what otherwise is a one-dimensional film. There seems to me to be a commentary on the idea of a Mainlander lost in Hong Kong being a country bumpkin, but depicted as a morally upstanding man with great kung fu skills; at once a criticism and a compliment. That his name is Swordsman is no joke, with his old school values like a Wuxia character.

The opening Kendo fight and the end one-on-one between Godenzi and Aurelio are so beautifully crafted that they top the face-off between the two in She Shoots Straight. Perhaps that film is better overall than License to Steal, but the combat in this movie is top class all the way. Both Godenzi and Aurelio have never looked better. Another rematch in the film is between Yuen and Billy Chow, and for pure choreography it tops the scene in Dragons Forever. In fact the last half an hour has endless rewatch-ability. Collin Chou's form and technique never looked better, as he takes on a bunch of heavies, and we are treated to a match between Yuen and him early in the film. While it's a bit short, there's no doubt we are seeing two of the greatest screen fighters go toe to toe

A hell of an entertaining 90 minutes, License to Steal misses out from being an absolute classic because a lot of the humour falls flat (the only laugh out loud moments for me come from bad subtitling, such as "Grimace at her like an onion"), and just how silly the film becomes towards the end, giving credence to the idea that Hong Kong movie scripts at the time were written on the set. The tonal shifts, which become part of the charm of Golden Age Hong Kong cinema, are here too jarring because the laughs don't work and parts of the film are a bit dead when there's no action going on. Yuen's performance is great, and as usual he gives his all. If you're looking for a film from the left field that contains action up there with the best from its actors, look no further.

My introduction to Yuen Baio came when I was 12, with the all-time 80s style action masterpiece Righting Wrongs. I'm not

gonna write about that here, watch this space for a piece dedicated to a movie that so many love. Shortly thereafter I picked up Millionaire's Express (called Shanghai Express on UK VHS), and fell more deeply in love with golden age Hong Kong cinema. Revered as one of the best action comedies ever made, Sammo Hung gathered together an unforgettable cast to make an unforgettable movie, one that I've watched countless times. The recent Eureka! Blu Ray release is a must for fans, as it includes both international and Chinese cuts of the film, AND a hybrid cut that combines both! It's great times for Hong Kong cinema fans.

The opening scene sets the comedic and action-packed tone as Sammo is first given a mop as a wig by soldiers, blows them all up with hand grenades, then is captured by Kenny Bee's bounty hunter, all set and shot in a snowy wasteland. Sammo himself said he almost froze to death in the snow as he only wears a pair of undies! Set in the early 20th century, the action moves to Sammo's sleepy hometown, where Eric Tsang is police chief and Yuen the chief firefighter. The whole town was a set on the Golden Harvest lot, and cost huge amounts for a Hong Kong film of the time. Unfortunately the film flopped in Hong Kong, something that is difficult to understand. To this day, it's one of the most entertaining movies of its time right up there with Project A and Police Story.

Millionaire's Express features a who's who of Hong Kong cinema at the time, with notable omissions like Chow Yun Fat and Andy Lau. Such was Sammo's pull that great film-makers like Corey Yuen Kwai heeded the call for cameos. The countless list of cameos includes my favourite Jimmy Wang Yu as Wong Kei Ying, playing the father of the legendary Wong Fei Hung, here depicted as a small child. He travels on the train with Shek Kin who plays another old master whose child challenges Wong Fei Hung, in a cute but brilliant kung fu fight in a train station. Hung discovered he could film in an old style train station in Thailand, and used a Thai steam train, for a reasonable price.

As Millionare's Express develops, it unleashes a vast ocean of explosive energy. Here we get slapstick comedy scenes led by the inimitable Richard Ng at his funniest, sight gags, Eric Tsang on stilts robbing a bank, silent movie sped up stunts and great one-liners. For the most part Sammo

and Yuen are at odds in the story, and when their showdown arrives mid-film it doesn't disappoint, with innovation and impact. The final reel is where the gold really lies, and the match ups are positively mouth-watering, with none of them disappointing.

Yukari Oshima is my favourite female golden age actress, and here is her first Hong Kong film role after breaking through in Taiwanese movies. One of them, A Book of Heroes, is an unsung gem. She plays a Samurai transporting a map, and is joined by Yasuaki Kurata, and the crew is led by Hwang Jang Lee. Three legends, and they are given ample opportunity to flex their fighting muscles. Yukari takes on thugs and walks up a wall; Kurata fights Richard Norton in which Norton again uses his catchphrase, originating from Twinkle, Twinkle Lucky Stars: painful? After a powerful kick. Hwang fights lackeys in a superb display of his bootwork.

The two on-on-ones deliver with aplomb. Yuen Baio fought Dick Wei numerous times onscreen, with another great bout in the picture Rosa, but here the exchanges, acrobatic moves from Baio and invention in film-making and choreography are through the roof. Sammo takes on Rothrock in the only duel the two had, and Rothrock said Hung's control was such that she knew he wouldn't hit her, a testament to the great man. And all this is without mentioning an ace comedic

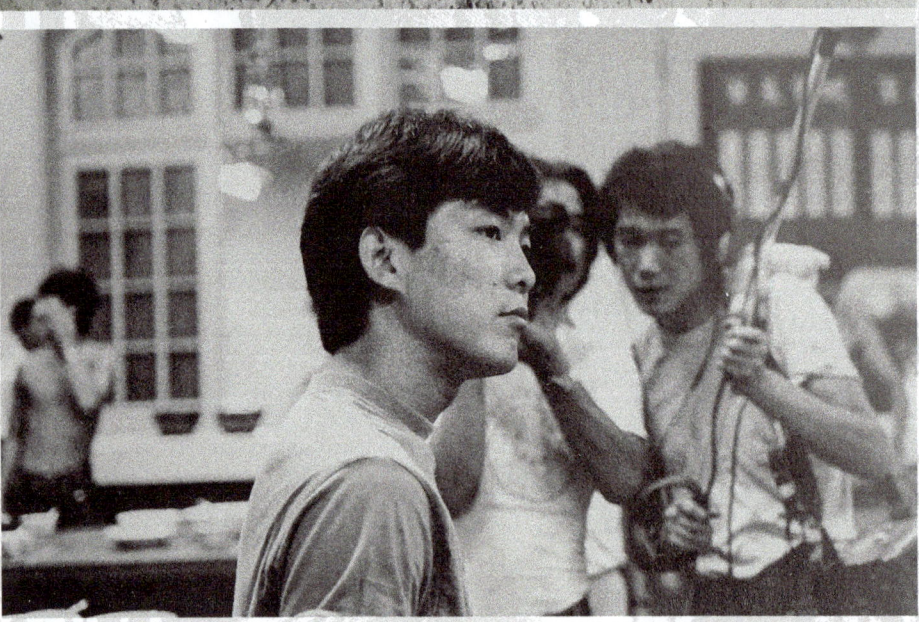

Eastern Condors (1990)

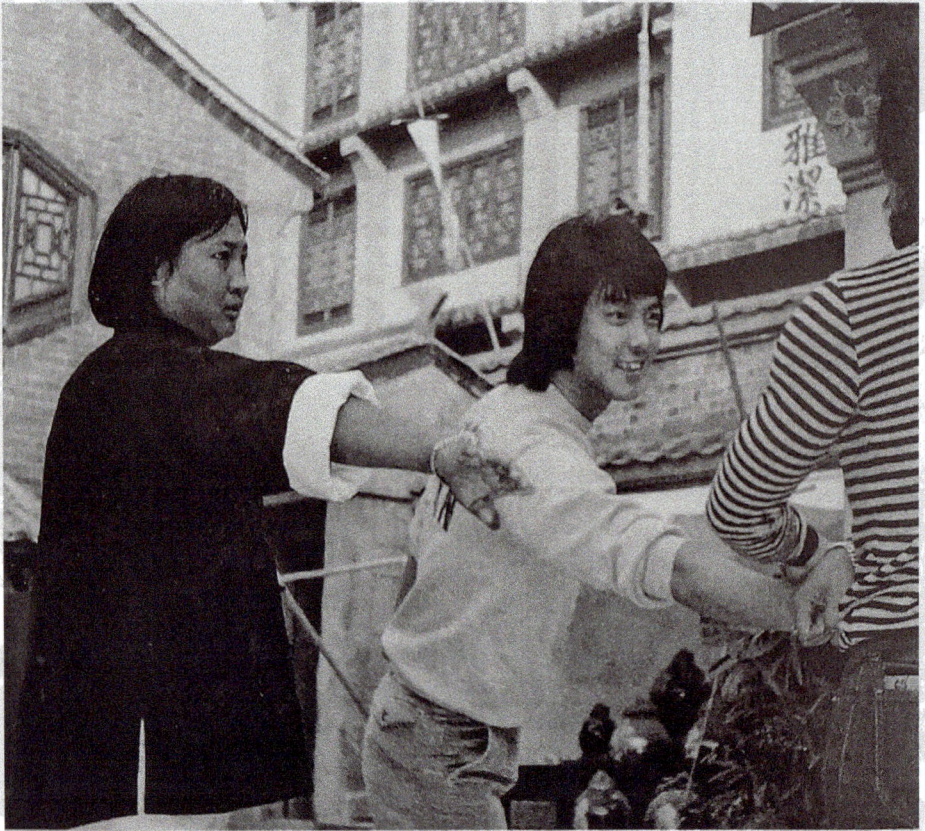

fight featuring Johnny Wang Lung Wei vs Meng Hoi and Hsaio Hou, Kenny Bee and Sammo ripping it up with a portable machine gun and Corey Yuen fighting with a ciggie dangling from his mouth. Millionare's Express is prime golden age Hong Kong cinema entertainment, and bar a few lines of dialogue that date the film and a plotline that can be hard to understand at the best of times, it's up there with the greatest.

Though Baio is no longer really active in the film industry, he still looks spritely and younger than his years as evidenced in his recent part in the movie Heroes Return. There are many other films to recommend that show off Yuen at his best, with some of my picks being Knockabout, his first starring role under the watchful eye of Sammo Hung, Shanghai, Shanghai which features the best fight between the two opera brothers, Iceman Cometh which is coming soon from 88 Films and Kid From Tibet, Yuen's directorial debut

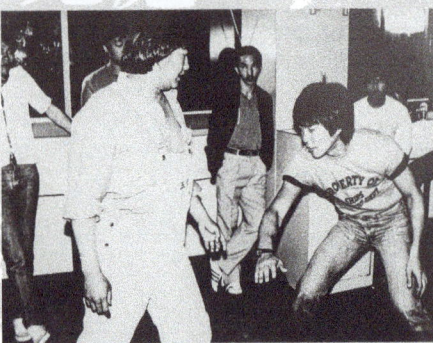

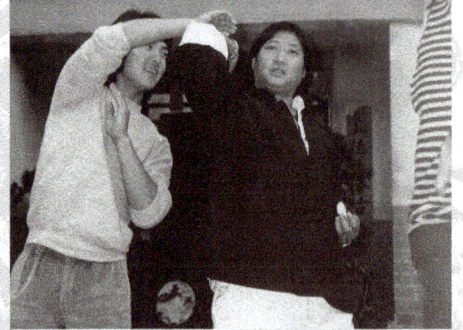

ENTER THE BLACK DRAGON

Interview with Ron Van Clief by Jason Mcneil

The year was 1973, and even as the movie-going and pop culture world was going crazy for kung-fu in the wake of Bruce Lee's simultaneous leap to international superstardom and untimely demise, up and coming film producer Serafim Karalexis had what he felt was a clear vision of things to come. Whether is was a "Paul on the Road to Damascas" moment of prophesy, what recovering alcoholics refer to as a "Moment of Clarity" or merely the clear-eyed and spot-on instincts of a producer in tune with the zeitgeist, Karalexis knew one thing and knew it for certain: the future of kung-fu cinema lay with non-Caucasians.

"The whites were no longer there," he said in a 1982 interview. "Blacks, Puerto Ricans, Chicanos [and] Orientals" would carry kung-fu movies to the next level, both in the ticket-buying audience and onscreen. "And since no Hong Kong film would have a Black hero, I realized that I was going to have to produce the film myself."

So strong was Karalexis' belief in his vision of the future of martial arts cinema, he ended his relationship with United International Pictures, moved to New York and started looking for "a Black actor who could do kung fu." Almost 200 actors answered Serafim's call, but none had the combination of charisma, martial arts mastery and soul brother funkiness that he was looking for – until Ron Van Clief strode boldly into the producer's office and unleashed a lightening fast kick that nearly scraped the ceiling – while wearing platform shoes, no less!

Funky footwear aside, Ron Van Clief was possessed of more real-world martial arts badassery than most wanna-be action heroes had even dreamed of! A black belt who had trained in Shotokan Karate, Hakko-ryu Jujitsu and Kendo, he was also an ex-Marine who, while training at Camp Lejeune in Jacksonville, North Carolina, had been arrested for refusing to sit in the back of a bus (at the height of Jim Crow Era Southern Segregation) and even escaped an attempted lynching (!!!) If ever a Black Action Hero was ready to stand up to Whitey and tell the Man where to stick it, it was the 31 year old Ron Van Clief!

Not incidentally, RVC, in addition to working as a bouncer at various dives and night spots in New York City (one memorable night fighting off 20 bikers with only the help of the club doorman), had learned the ins and outs of movie stunt work from Frank Sinatra's fight double, Alex Stevens, and had even done a bit of work on The Anderson Tapes (1971) and Shaft (Can you dig it?)

Karalexis had found his man. In very short order, Ron Van Clief was on a plane, bound for East Asia.

While Serafim remained behind in New York, RVC found himself in the midst of a co-production that was not at all what he (or, apparently, Karalexis) had expected.

"They didn't even know I was a martial artist!" Van Clief says. "They were all like: 'Do you think you could maybe kick, here?

Oh, wow! That's a good kick! We didn't know you could kick so well!'"

The resulting film, originally titled Tough Guy and starring Jason Pai Piao, and retitled The Black Dragon for US theatrical release, is a bit of a mixed bag and, while action packed from beginning to end, can be a bit confusing to first-time viewers, as Ron Van Clief is barely in the first half of the film!

Comparisons have been drawn – and not unfairly – to The Big Boss (1971), wherein Bruce Lee was something of a secondary character for the first part of the film, mostly just standing around while others chewed scenery, until someone in charge apparently recognized what they had in front of their cameras and turned the Little Dragon loose to work his martial arts magic and steal the second half of the film!

In a similar fashion, Ron Van Clief's role grows larger and larger as the film rolls on, and by the end he is obviously the Ass-Kicker in Chief right up until the end credits! Sorry, Jason Pai Piao, but the Black Dragon just blew you off the screen!

Although there are several standout martial arts moments in the film, perhaps the most striking (quite literally!) is that it is one of very few films – possibly the only one – wherein the "Final Fight" ends with a nut shot! (And one of a very VERY few kung fu ball busters that didn't somehow involve Bob Wall.....)

Released in America in 1974 as a "starring Ron Van Clief" film and with a recut trailer, featuring a funky voice-over by New York R&B radio disc jockey, Gerry Bledsoe, assuring audiences that there would be "none of that jumping around and lying thru the air, 'cause this is the real shit!" the movie hit big and went on to be one of the top 50 box office grossing movies of the year, with ticket sales over six million dollars!

To no one's surprise, more Black Dragon movies followed hot on its heels.

The following year, a martial arts documentary titled The Super Weapon was shot, "Starring Ron Van Clief" and featuring a number of the biggest names in 1970s martial arts, including Charles

BD-2
RON VAN CLIEF
JASON PAI POW
JORGE ESTRAGA
THE BLACK DRAGON
A MADISON WORLD FILM
IN COLOR R

RON VAN CLIEF
THE 4 TIMES WORLD CHAMPION!
CHARLES La Pantera BONET
THE BLACK DRAGON'S REVENGE

THE SUPER WEAPON
RON VAN CLIEF

BRUCE RHEE
RON VAN CLIEF
CATCH BRUCE LEE FEVER
YANGTZE PRODUCTIONS LIMITED PRESENTS
Kungfu Fever
BILL STANLEY STEVEN CHOW MAY LEE
An AQUARIUS FILMS Release

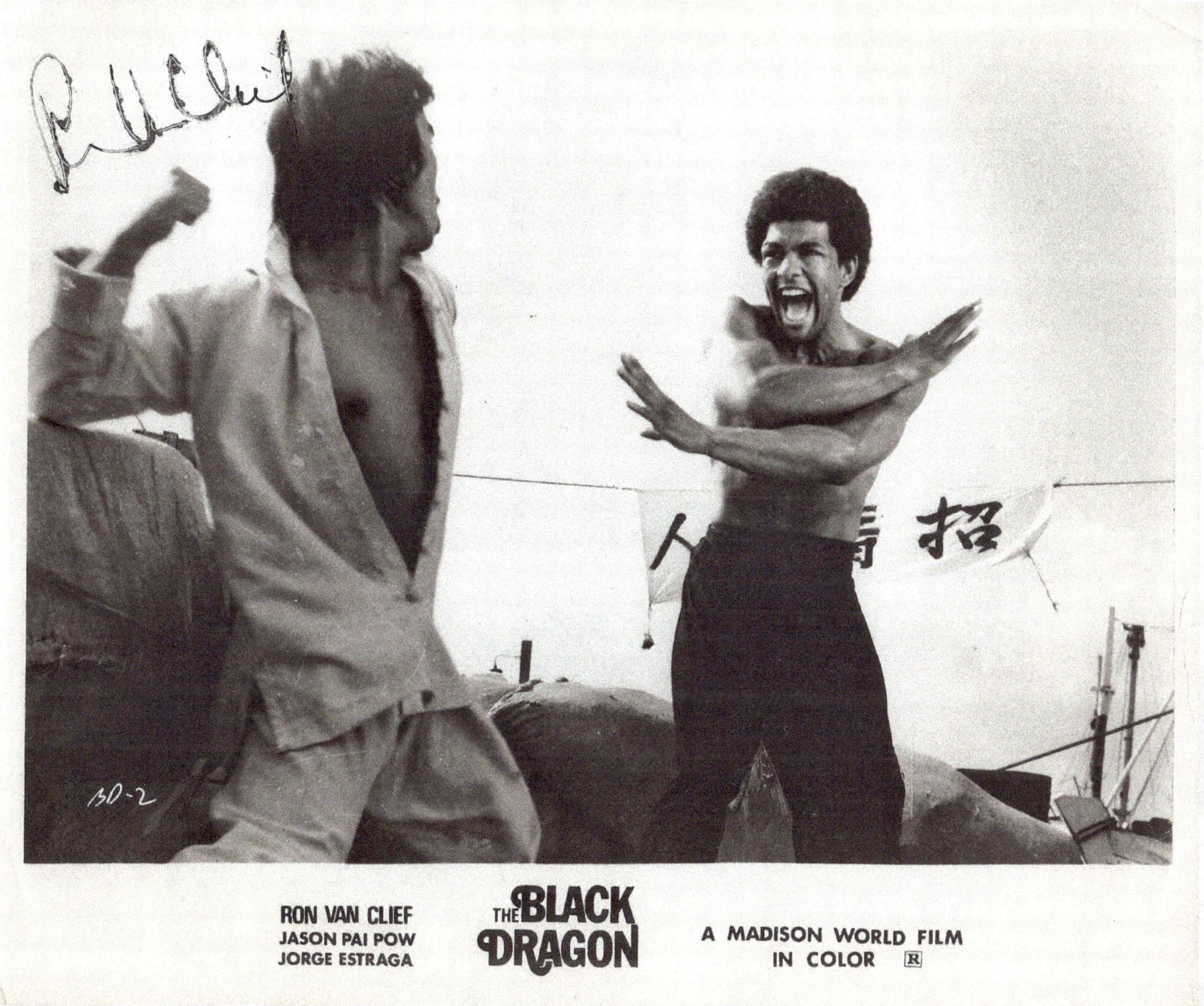

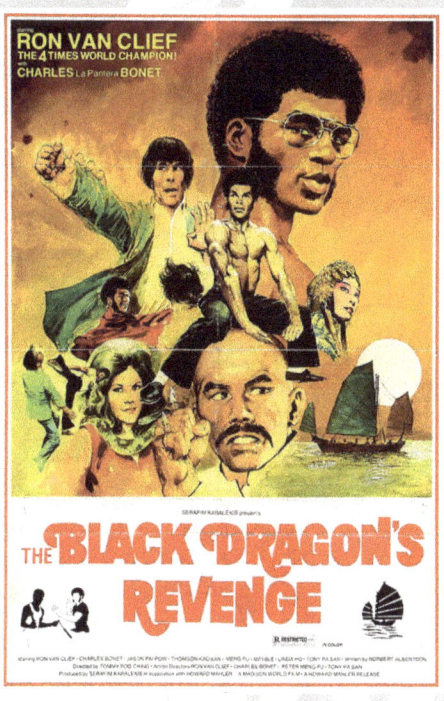

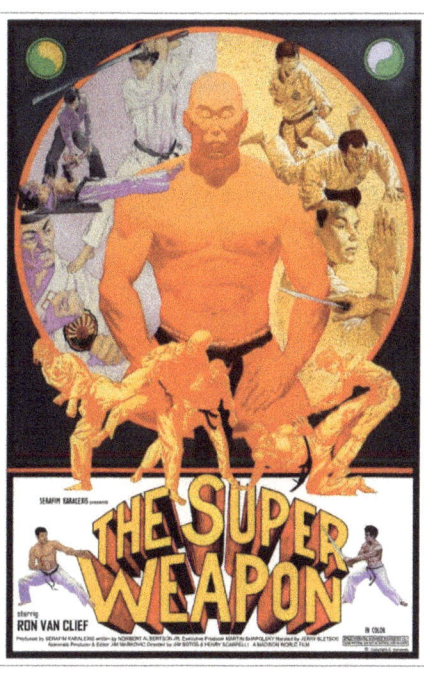

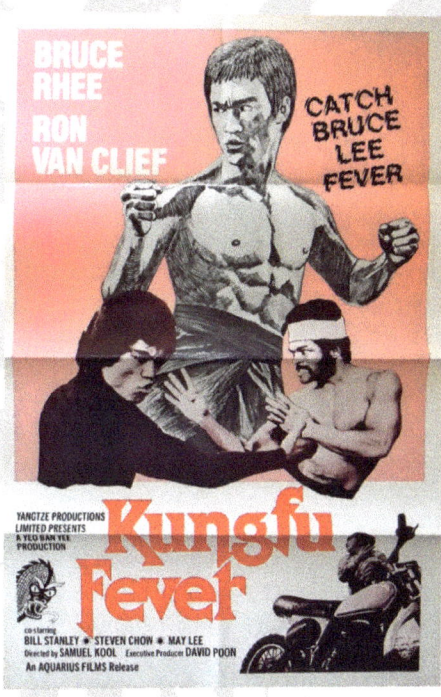

Bonet, an old training partner and friend of Van Clief's from their military days.

"Charles Bonet and I were stationed together in the Marines," says RVC, "and he introduced me to some of the masters we ended up training with! Charlie and I go way back, and his martial arts skills were no joke! He was the real deal!"

Perhaps seeking to continue with his notion that "Blacks, Puerto Ricans, Chicanos [and] Orientals" were the future of kung fu cinema, Serafim Karalexis decided to cast Van Clief and Charles Bonet together in The Black Dragon's Revenge (aka The Death of Bruce Lee), released in 1975.

In addition to the return of the Black Dragon (whose character name is simply "Ron Van Clief" and who sports a T-shirt advertising his own dojo onscreen), The Black Dragon's Revenge offers viewers RVC and "La Pantiera" ("The Latin Panther") Charles Bonet, as private investigators, scouring the streets, alleys and antique stores (!!!) of Hong Kong, trying to find the truth behind the death of Bruce Lee.

Its a classic bit of peak Brucesploitation, even including the mandatory photo of Bruce Lee in his coffin, and a seemingly endless series of kung fu thugs jumping out of alleyways and from behind bushes and trees, just fighting and fighting and more and more glorious fighting – including an appearance by Qiu Yuen (whom younger readers will know best as the Land Lady in Kung Fu Hustle) and a mountaintop free-for-all that shows off RVC's prodigious kicking skills as well as a very snazzy oversized pair of chain nunchaku! (Personal Note: If anyone knows what prop box or stunt coordinator's home dojo those 'chuks ended up in, please contact this writer via Eastern Heroes. They need to be hung in a place of honor – after being gratuitously twirled a whole bunch by yours truly! Anyway, back to the movie....)

In fact, there"s so much kung fu fighting in The Black Dragon's Revenge that we occasionally start to lose the plot: Ron Van Clief (as Ron Van Clief) has been hired to "solve" the mystery of Bruce Lee's death! Fear not, gentle reader, for the "Mystery" is revealed at the end of the flick.

And I quote: "In my search for the truth, I was told that the sky has unexpected clouds and storms. A man has sudden fortune and misfortune. Nothing depends on man's own dream. His whole life is arranged by fate. Nature needs no weapon to kill a man. As you know, there is only one way to be born, a hundred to die. On the path of death walk men of all ages, and you find out the universe is ruled by letting things alone."

Ohhhhkay, Old Sifu Dude. Thanks for clearing that up.

And then the credits roll.

The following year, The Super Weapon documentary was released with Van Clief, Bonet and a host of others. Its a fun watch, albeit leaning a bit more into legend and hyperbole than actual historical fact, and features some truly amazing performances from a "Who's Who" of Martial Arts movers and shakers in mid-70s North America. As of this writing, its available to view on about a dozen different streaming services, as they say, "free with commercials" and is well worth checking out.

Similarly, the 1980 "more or less a documentary" titled Fist of Fear, Touch of Death, which also stars Ron Van Clief, as well as Fred "The Hammer" Williamson and narrated/hosted by Adolph Caesar, is also worth checking out, if only for the delightfully bizarre combination of martial arts demonstrations with celebrity interviews giving their opinions about why and how Bruce Lee died. (Which I thought we had cleared up with the "Stoned College Sophomore Trying to Explain Nietzschean Existential Nihilism" above, but apparently not.....) combined with a truly bizarre melange of vintage footage.

Filmed in and around Aaron Banks' 1979 "Oriental World of Self-Defense" martial arts expo and tournament, then cobbled together with footage from Bruce Lee's early, childhood films and some samurai movie footage supposedly chronicling the Bushido exploits of the Very Little Dragon's Japanese grandfather (???), the flick finally hodge-podges its way back to Madison Square Garden where one Louis Neglia, the winner of the tournament's final two round kickboxing match, has earned the right to be "Bruce Lee's

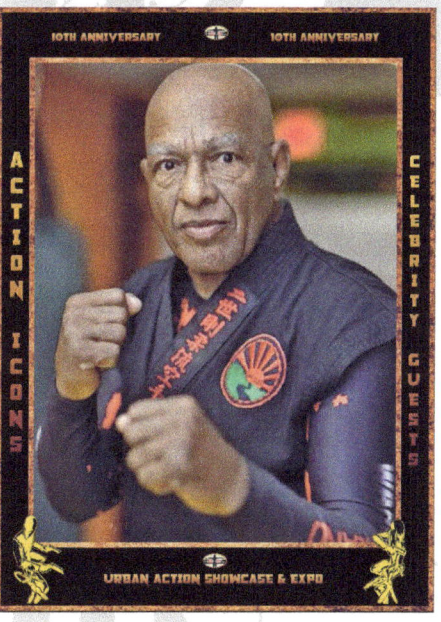

Don't Miss
This Opportunity
to Train with
a Legend!
VAN CLIEF
THE BLACK DRAGON
RON VAN CLIEF
CHINESE GOJU
AND
AIKIJITSU SEMINAR
SATURDAY, JULY 13, 2013
11:00 AM - 1:00 PM
MAKATO SCHOOL OF MARTIAL ARTS
89 Main Street
Fair Haven, Vermont
TRAINING FOR LIFE!
5 Time WORLD KARATE CHAMPION
15 Time ALL-AMERICAN CHAMPION

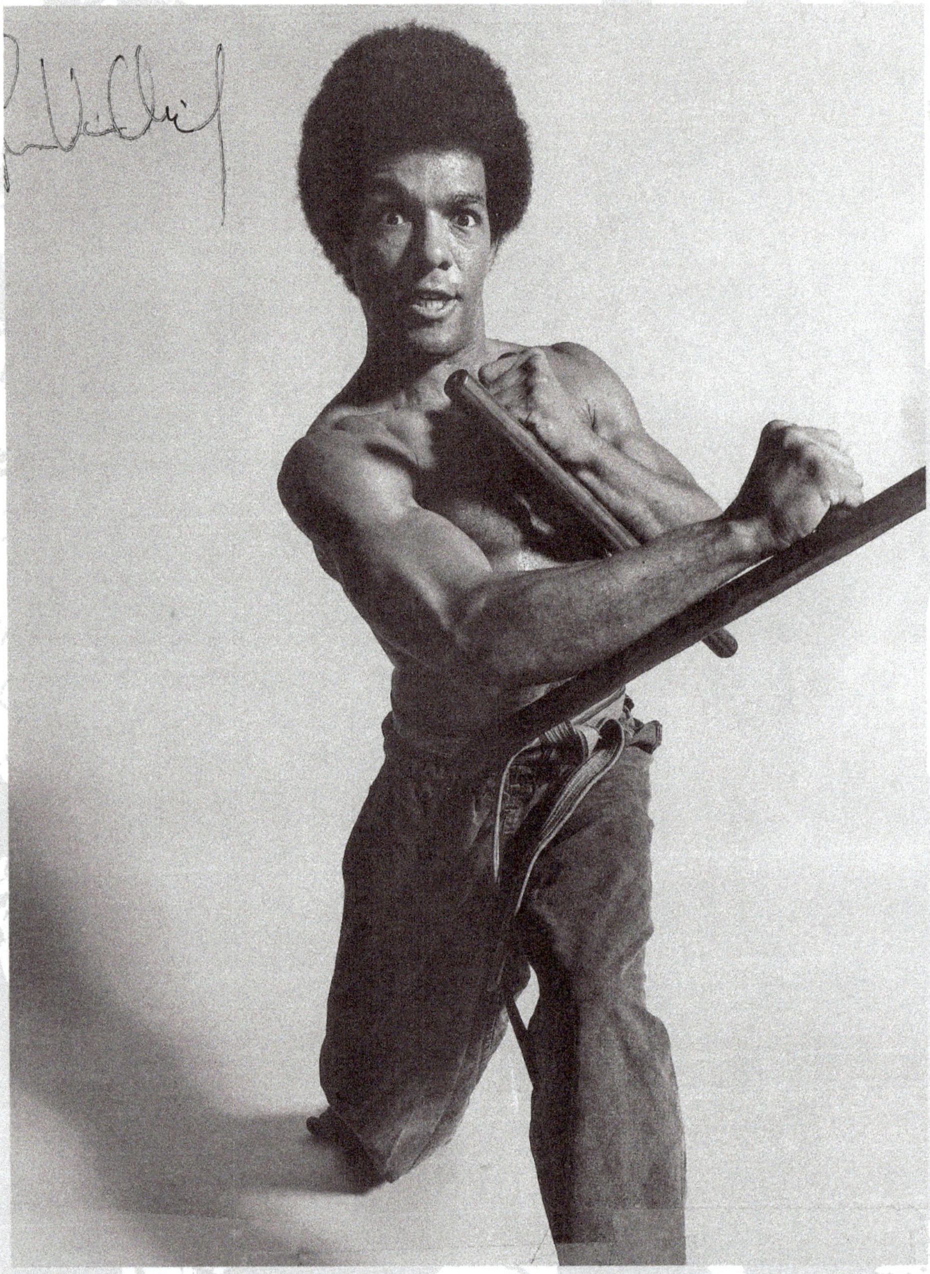

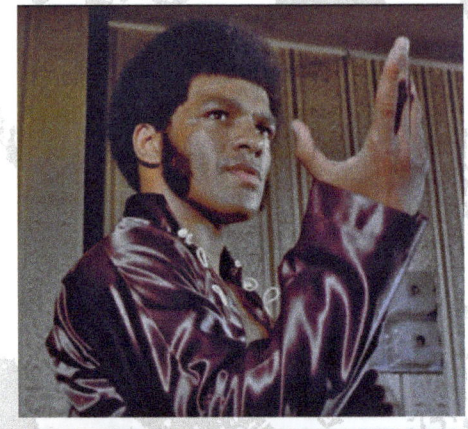

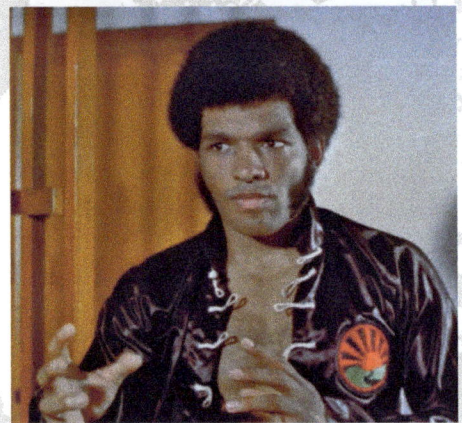

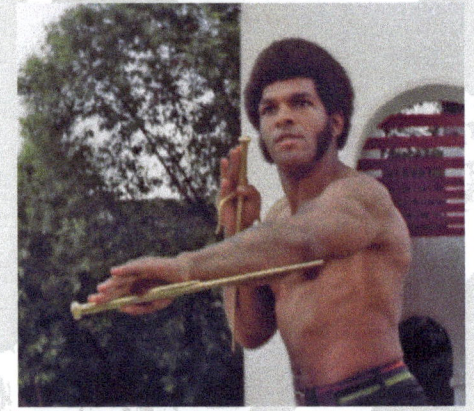

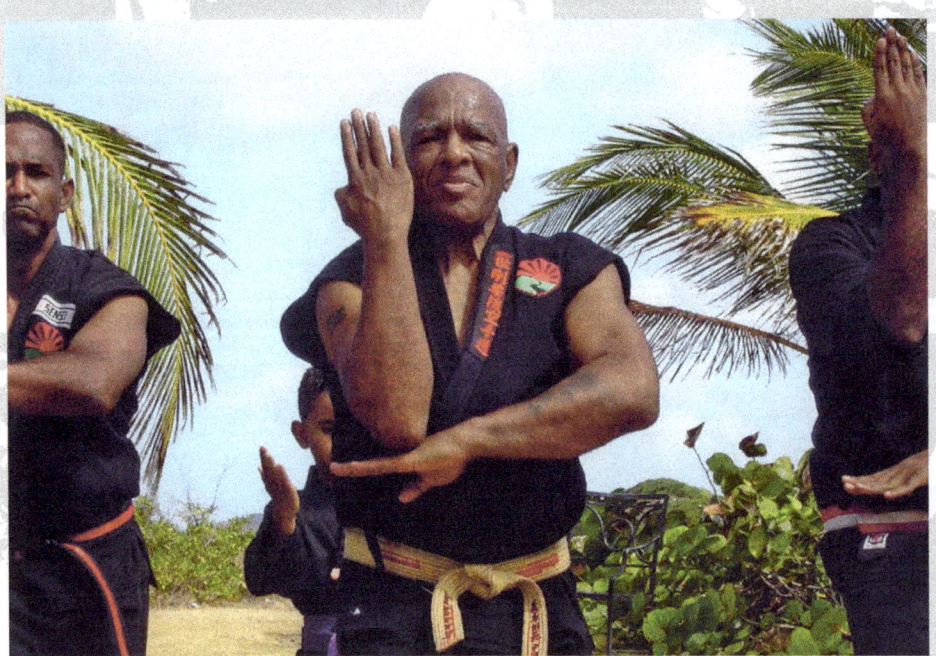

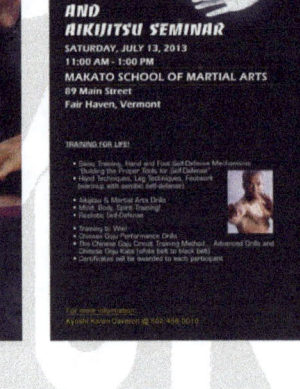

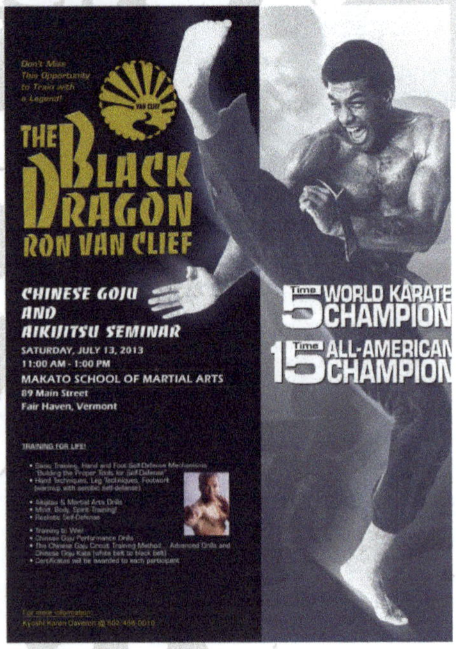

Successor!" (No, I've never heard of him, either. I guess the title didn't stick.)

As the 1970s drew to an end, so too did both the kung fu movie and Blaxpoitation movie crazes (with the notable exception of 1985's The Last Dragon), and Ron Van Clief moved on to bigger, better, and occasionally greener (as in cash money green) pastures!

In addition to running 17 - 20 dojos simultaneously and teaching self-defense and fighting techniques to the United States Secret Service in a training hall located underneath the World Trade Center from 1983 – 1993 (for which he earned a Special Commendation), Van Clief was always on the cutting edge of whatever was hot in the ever-changing martial arts world, hitching his wagon for awhile to the Ninjamania of the 80s and even diving headfirst into Mixed Martial Arts in the 1990s, fighting in the Ultimate Fighting Championship against Royce Gracie in UFC 4 at age 51!

Even now at 79 years of age, Grandmaster Ron Van Clief prides himself on continuing to grow, create and always strive for new levels of excellence.

"Every day," he says, "I wake up and have the opportunity to be better than I was the day before. There is no better challenge in life than that."

About the Author:

Jason McNeil is an actor, writer and martial artist who has appeared in numerous movies and television shows, including as host of Stars-Stunts-Action! - taking you behind the scenes of action movies and martial arts entertainment, now streaming on Tubi! He also once got to meet the late, great Bob Wall, but did not, as so many of his martial arts heroes did before him, get to kick Bob in.

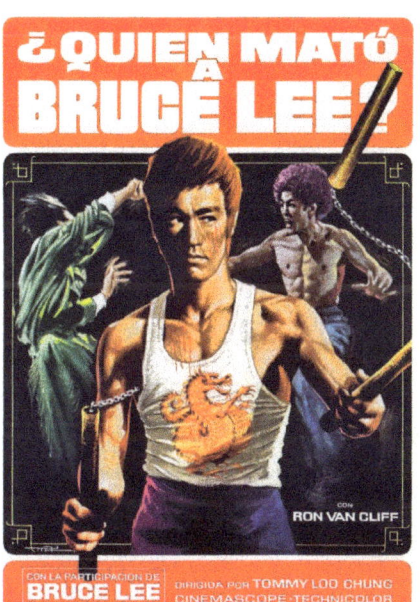

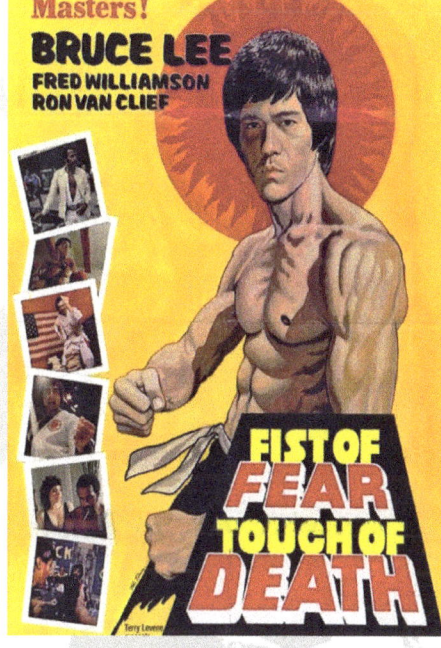

REVENGEANCE
Death Games & Angry Ranger
By Shazad Asghar

Death Games and Angry Ranger are both highly regarded by kung fu movie fans for featuring some of the best action of the 90s. Originally seen on VHS and VCD copies, both films were often mentioned online in the early 2000s by fans on websites and forums. Angry Ranger was released by Joy Sales in a remastered DVD format, but Death Games does not have any recent official release.

Death Games (1997) was a Taiwanese production and starred Fan Siu Wong (aka Louis Fan), son of actor Fan Mei-Sheng, with action overseen by Lin Wan-Chang, who worked on numerous films, including A Book of Heroes and the Kung Fu

Kids series. Fan Siu Wong was the young witness to a crime in the Yuen Biao classic Righting Wrongs, aka Above the Law, and would later be better known in the west for starring in Riki-Oh/The Story of Ricky. For a while he moved onto TV roles between film work, including starring in the series Fist of Power with Moon Lee. He would later turn up in Ip Man amongst other films, and is working to this day.

Angry Ranger (1991) starred Ben Lam Kwok-Bun and was directed by Wang Lung Wei (aka Johnny Wang), the Shaw Brothers veteran who has an extensive filmography as an actor and also directed a handful of films. Angry Ranger is a Jackie Chan Stunt Team production. Ben Lam was often cast as a villain, or in a supporting role, but Angry Ranger allowed him to demonstrate the skills and charisma he possessed in a leading role. He was one of the villains in Police Story 2 and has a memorable role in Donnie Yen's Legend of the Wolf as the leader of the bandit gang. He also appeared later on in Donnie Yen's Flashpoint, but sadly in a smaller role.

Both films focus on themes of vengeance and revenge. Death Games has a villain of western origin who cannot move on from the loss of his parents and sibling decades ago, seeking revenge despite warnings from all around him. Angry Ranger is the tale of an anti-hero who has been engaged in gang fights for years, not giving in to the criminal element around him, while protecting his friends, but also putting himself and those around him at risk by incurring the wrath of the local gangsters. Death Games has a strong supporting cast, with Leung-Kar Yan in a non-fighting role, Ngai Sing (aka Colin Chou) as the effeminate ninja master, Long; and Kim Maree Penn as the crime boss Tiger's girlfriend, who is also a fighter working within his organisation. Billy Chow also appears as David, a master of Thai boxing decked out in camouflage gear, and a red headband topped Rambo-like look that is certainly distinctive, to say the least.

The film kicks things off with an intro sequence set in an outside location on a large flight of stairs, with Fan dressed in white versus an opponent in black clothing, and then cuts to a training sequence with multiple students of Fan's school attacking him simultaneously in a garden. The introduction has fast, quick-cut action, and is reminiscent of older films which would feature training scenes or a fight demo, often in front of a studio backdrop, as a taster for the kind

of action which would feature later on. This sequence really does set the scene and leaves the viewer anticipating some sharp action scenes. Some of the music cues seem taken from a couple of late 80s western martial arts flicks. The intro fights do have rapid hits but they are not obviously heavy on the undercranking. Some of the acrobatics are subtly doubled, but there are some great moments, like a flip descending the steps towards an opponent while the camera captures it from a first-person viewpoint. The kinetic feel of this intro, with multiple hits before cutting away, and long shots filmed from a reasonable distance, demonstrate the skill of the choreographers, performers and stunt team involved in this production. Although, obviously, a martial arts film focuses heavily on the fights, the film does have a storyline. A westerner named Tiger seeks revenge for his father (Lyon), his mother and young sister, who were unfortunately killed years ago, and Fu (Leung Kar-Yan) and his partner Tong had something to do with their death. Although the subtitles aren't the best, Lyon was a smuggler and Tong gave himself up to face jail, not allowing Fu to join him so he could raise both his and Tong's daughters together, which he does without informing them that they are not sisters. The girls are Min, Tong's girl and Jin/Jen, Fu's daughter. We are shown all of this in a flashback, to twenty years earlier, although it is not presented in the clearest manner and the biggest indicator is that Leung Kar-Yan's hair is not greying.

The film does have some flaws, mainly the scenes with the daughters being presented in a melodramatic manner that borders on cheesy, sometimes with their father Fu with references to pain and tragedy and the afterlife. This is in contrast to the westerner Shelly, who is depicted as a strong woman trying to follow a martial arts code. The main villain is also slightly one note, seeking revenge (perhaps understandably) and willing to alienate anyone in pursuit of his goal, including his partner Shelly, who is played with style by Kim Maree Penn. Although she is willing to aid him in his mission, she stresses to him the importance of patience and seems bound by honour. This is demonstrated when she lets Kau Hwa, Fan's character, escape a couple of times when she could easily have her henchmen gun him down. At one point she says to Tiger that if more and more deaths are needed, then that is certainly not what martial arts teach. Righteous actions and sacrifice are touched on in the film's plot, with Shelly asking Kau at one point why he involves himself in this situation. Although she isn't aware that Tong looked after Kau's father in jail, he states that it is for righteous reasons he is willing to intervene, and that how this is viewed and acted upon is different in Eastern and Western cultures. It could be argued that Tiger is a character without morals and driven by the pain of being orphaned. The way Shelly is presented as a character could be seen as the film attempting to not demonize or

stereotype all westerners, as she seems to respect Kau for his philosophy and morals. Shelly and Kau have a couple of fights, with the former asking the latter to teach her how to defeat him. They display a respect for each other despite their differences, and it is refreshing to see that the filmmakers didn't resort to making it a love triangle. The last thirty minutes feature a fair amount of fight scenes, with the exaggerated macho character played by Billy Chow contrasted with the effeminate ninja in Japanese robes, Lone, played by Ngai Sing. He seems to really enjoy the role, breaking into mischievous expressions while accompanied by his two female companions. The fight between Lone and Kau stops and starts, with some serious kicking action unleashed. Fan Siu Wong breaks into a Bruce Lee stance at times during these parts of the film, and his tracksuit bottoms could be referencing Game of Death, as could the film's English title. Finally, I must mention that a fair amount of weapons are thrown into the mix, as well as hand to hand combat, so the fights remain varied and enjoyable at all times.

Angry Ranger has a strong ex-Shaw Brothers presence, with Wang Lung Wei directing, and a surprise appearance from Sun Chien of the Venoms crew as a vicious triad boss. Cheung Kwok-Wah, as opposing boss Macau Hua, and Benny Lai are present as one of the first boss's crew. Sun Chien plays Big Circle Han, a mob boss with interests in gambling and an assortment of other illegal activities. He has a young woman captive, Jane, who he invited to Hong Kong by initially acting as a concerned elder, before keeping her trapped in a loveless relationship, attempting to make up for her isolation (she is followed everywhere by his men) and loneliness, with material objects.

Ben Lam plays the character of Peter, who has been in prison for a while due to gang activity, a fight that involved him defending his friend Chen Hsing. While Peter was gone, Hsing has gone onto success with a car business and also a news stand that is run by his younger brother. Hsing also attends English classes, making moves on the tutor he has an eye on. We first see Peter as he steps off a bus, top with sleeves rolled up, the same way he wears his jackets, with a Miami Vice gangster look. As he tears the filter off his cigarette before lighting it, the message seems to be, Peter does not mess around. Although it's a brief scene. If 'Bad to the Bone' were playing in the background, like in Terminator 2 when we see Schwarzenegger begin his mission, it would probably set the mood adequately.

Our anti-hero is initially avoiding trouble in the local area, letting the junior gangsters' provocations slide. He visits a local elder's shop, and the uncle informs him the world has become more degenerate, due to the local rascals. Seeing

a butcher's blade cutting meat triggers a flashback: we witness Ben Lam's character tooling up with a blade and wrapping his fist, to help his friend Hsing who is already being attacked by a large group. The flashback indicates to the audience that Peter is handy with a blade and his fists, but then we hear sirens, and everyone runs, including his friend. Yet our hero stays to keep roughing up an opponent, and then surrenders to the police. Peter never ran and never will - similar in outlook to a politician at an illegal COVID lockdown gathering.

Hsing's young brother, Hsi B, greets Peter and mentions that they won't be bullied anymore now that he is back in town. The lad's grandmother welcomes a confused Peter back from his travels with the navy. Hsi B is wearing a top with a large Batman logo. This is likely because the original Tim Burton film was a huge hit, and is referenced in some Hong Kong films of the time. The kid does refer to the bullying they endured while Peter was detained under the care of HMP Rebels Without Pause, but later the kid will realise that good old Peter may get them all killed as well as himself.

At times Hsing, with his glasses, looks like he could double Yuen Biao during his Righting Wrongs/Above the Law period. Soon we see a local disco or dancehall, with a DJ wearing glasses with small lights on each end. The setup couldn't look more 80s if they tried. A girl is shown dancing, from the back, standing out because she has a white dress on. The local ruffians are ever-present, even at the disco, posing like fat cats while surrounded by the girls they constantly mistreat. Ben Lam's character notices the girl in the dress - knowing his luck, what are the odds that she's trapped as a captive in a relationship with a gang boss who was once a deadly venom? Throughout the film, the viewer should ask the question, 'Does Peter care?' Does Peter care about kicking off with the junior gangsters? Does Peter care that this pretty lady may lead to huge trouble? Does Peter care that he may end up killing someone eventually, or risk his own life? The answer is usually NO, Peter wants to care, but struggles with these things because he's Peter.

Gazing across the smokey dancefloor at the pretty woman, who is dancing like an extra in a Madonna video, Ben Lam has a look on his face that seems to say, 'Maybe I would risk losing my freedom to be with her, perhaps grab a blade and tear some limbs like the good old/bad old 80s.' This scene is super 80s in nature, from the music to the clothing, although it was released in the early 90s. The two make a great couple, as Peter takes her hand to dance, and soon the crowd part for them, stopping to clap, while they dance and the DJ gets busy in the back with his illuminating eyewear, as the bad guys begin to notice. One of Han's men asks, "Who is this dunce?" At that moment Peter's younger friend realises that he may soon get them a free one-way ticket to the afterlife.

Later we learn Peter's sister (perhaps his cousin, it's never been quite clear to me – but I am a bit slow), is working as a hostess at a nightclub, having to accompany older men. She helps Peter and tells him to go to work at their Uncle's store on the seafood section. When alone, she cries as she also seems stuck in a situation that is far from ideal. Jane, the girl in the dress, turns up at the stall Peter works on, followed everywhere by her thuggish minders. Later, she and Peter escape to spend some time together, but Han will punish her for this, and assaults her physically and in the bedroom. Somehow, after having stolen a villain's car for a joyride, and being with Jane, Peter has offended both of the local gangs. His friends and family's businesses are targeted, and things will come to a head sooner rather than later. At one point, replying to his friend's advice to let certain wrongdoings slide, as he can't kill everyone, Peter replies that he can't turn a blind eye, and that he was born in this place and will die in this place.

There are two fight scenes that stand out in particular. The first is when Ben Lam goes to a small local spot to punish some of the lower ranked gangsters, the 'Shangri-La Lounge.' He stops across the road to gather his thoughts for a second, before he enters and gets to work. Taking on the hoods with a barrage of kicks and punches, many times his knee seems to connect to a skull. There is some great stunt work where someone is sent flying through the glass section of a door. It's one of those moments where you instantly feel for the stuntman, if you have a heart that is. This scene is short but expertly put together. It is the JC Stunt Team after all, and could have been a fight from one of the first two Police Story films.

Another fight has Peter take on Macau Hua, the other gang boss played by Cheung Kwok-Wah. This scene takes place in the town at night, when Peter is enraged after what some of the thugs have done to his loved ones, and he quickly dispatches Hua's men while incensed, before the boss intervenes. Macau Hua and Peter fight but show respect to each other. The scene is shot from several angles, including an aerial shot. The quality of the fight and the way they trade blows while in their stances almost reminds me of the end to Martial Club, which, of course, featured the director of this film in a clash with Gordon Liu. Also, Sun Chien, as Big Circle Han, with his spikey 80s hairstyle, gold jewels and smart/casual attire, has a look that maxes out the evil crime boss fashion meter. He would have fitted nicely in Scarface, perhaps as an importer of rare powders. Later in the film, Benny Lai pops up as one of Han's

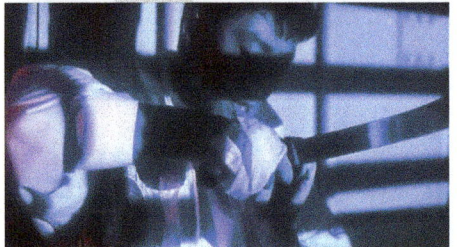 

men. He is easily recognisable for his role in Police Story 2 as one of the gang along with Ben Lam, although in this film they are on opposing sides.

I would argue that both films have their flaws, but the action in both has touches of the best fights filmed during the early 90s and then the latter part of the decade. Both Death Games and Angry Ranger leave the viewer wanting more, with quite a few short and explosive action sequences in both. Death Games falls into cheesy melodrama at times. The storytelling and structure of Death Games is flawed, and perhaps lets the action side down. Angry Ranger has some excellent fight scenes which make one wish for more. If only they were perhaps better spaced-out through the film. The ending action is quite chaotic and perhaps not the best climax considering what has come before. It has a dark tone throughout, perhaps fatalistic. It is not bleak, but it presents the lead character as being unable to avoid trouble for himself and his loved ones. He takes risks without a second thought, and although it is admirable that he does not bow down to the villains, he is more tragic in many ways than simply an action anti-hero. If you haven't seen these films and alike 90s productions, I would highly recommend them. If you have seen them already, maybe give them another viewing. It would be a welcome surprise to see these films released again and given a quality presentation, as many cult titles get ignored or overlooked due to rights issues or other factors, resigned to remain in video limbo.

KWAN TAK HING
By Dave Cater

Kwan Tak-Hing is best-known to kung fu film fans for having played legendary martial arts master Wong Fei Hung in damned-near a hundred movies! But there was much, much more to the man than just his action-packed and prolific acting career, as Dave Cater found out when he got the chance to sit down and talk with the Great Man in 1986 at a martial arts tournament that was one of several stops on an American tour!

FUN FACT: As Kwan Tak-Hing spoke very little English and Cater even less Chinese, the conversation/interview was translated back and forth by none other than the brother of the Little Dragon, ROBERT LEE!

Read on for a full account of all the very interesting, informative an often unexpected stuff that Kwan Tak-Hing had to say near the end of his extraordinary career (and a decade before his passing in 1996.)

To millions of Chinese moviegoers, he was Wong Fei Hung. But to a handful of guerrilla fighters, he was the spirit of freedom.
Kwan Tak-Hing was the Bob Hope of Chinese theater. In the late 1930's, Kwan organized a theatrical troupe that entertained front-line fighters during the most furious period of the Sino-Japanese war.

Several things, however, separated Kwan from his American counterpart. While Hope carried a golf club and traveled in relative style (for wartime, that is), Kwan was forced to carry a loaded gun and usually camped out under the stars in areas so remote the troupe sometimes went several days without food.

And, most importantly, the enemy never placed a price on Hope's head. Kwan was not so lucky. His contribution to the spirit of the Chinese cause was considered so

great, the Japanese offered a bounty of $40,000 for his capture.

"I wasn't really worried," Kwan said.

"The guerrilla fighters would protect me during the performances. The enemy was only about ten miles away," Kwan added.

The Japanese, Kwan explained, hoped to persuade him to change sides. "They wanted to use me for their propaganda," he said. "I knew I wouldn't do that. I would rather die." Rather than cower under the mounting Japanese presence, Kwan grew stronger and pushed his troupe forward, raising the spirits of the Chinese warriors.

Although his steadfast courage earned him his country's heartfelt thanks, he gained real respect through his continuous portrayal of legendary Chinese martial artist Wong Fei Hung. In the 30 years following the Sino-Japanese War, Kwan played Wong Fei Hung in 98 movies and 13 television episodes. So powerful was Kwan's recreation of Hung, whose life was immortalized in the book, The Legend of Wong Fei Hung, that the actor seldom was called by his real name.
Little is known about thee real Wong Fei Hung. According to records, he was born in 1847 in Xiqiao village, Nanhai county in Guangdong province. Known as one of the province's best lion dancers, Wong was also proficient in the Iron Wire Fist, Five Forms Fist, Tiger Vanishing Fist and Shadowless Kick forms of kung-fu.

Kwan's acting was so convincing, Wong's wife once said, "You're just like him." According to Kwan, who at 82 could have passed for a man 30 years his younger, playing the same character in almost 100 movies was a continuous learning experience. At no time, he insisted, did the character become boring.

"The more movies I made, the more ambitious or energetic I got," he admitted. "The philosophy was always good." Kwan's film popularity came because he was both a fine martial artist and trained actor. And his weapons prowess was unparalleled. Some of his movie weapons included the long bench at a restaurant, supporting bamboo used by the coolies, iron hooks, umbrellas and floor sweepers.

But his favorite weapon may have been the whip, which he first discovered on a trip to the United States in 1932. A fan of cowboy movies, Kwan was

given an 18 foot whip as a gift during an acting tour of San Francisco. He practiced in the basement of his living quarters for the next 14 months and became so proficient, he once extinguished the flames on 104 of 110 candles with the tip of his whip.

In one scene from a Wong Fei Hung movie, Kwan was surrounded by 20 men holding bundles of flames. Using his whip, Kwan put out the bundles.

In addition to his exotic weapons and acting skills, Kwan was adapt at a number of traditional kung-fu styles as well. He practiced the "Ten Forms" (snake, dragon, leopard, tiger, crane, lion, elephant, monkey, tiger cat and horse) and gong yau kuen, patterns containing "over a thousand movements ranging from flexibility to forcefulness."

Like Wong Fei Hung, Kwan also had a talent for lion dancing. He gained inspiration for his movements from watching newborn cats! "You dangle something in front of them, they'll paw at it then retreat," he noted. Creeping low, Kwan moved his eyes from side to side, his hands near his cheeks to recreate the movements of the paws.

"The various moods of the lion dance," he said, "have the joy of green-picking, when the lion first catches sight of the green, the fury, then the green is not easy to get, the sadness, when the lion feels despair, and the ecstasy, when it gets hold of thee green." Kwan said the true lion dancer must be both "as active as a rabbit out of grasp" and "as serene and quiet as a maiden."

Above all else, Kwan Tak-Hing was a true believer in Chinese tradition. When, at age 53, he discovered the beauty of Chinese calligraphy, he immediately studied the Lam-Chi-Yun temple script for six months and then learned the style of Cheung Yuk Wai for two years. By the end of his life, each word he brushed was said to be valued at ten thousand Chinese dollars!

But there was a side to Kwan that few knew. When his mother took ill, Kwan followed the example of Chan Pak Sha, whose virtues of "honesty, faithfulness, filial piety and righteousness" made him a saint in Chinese folklore. After his mother's death, Kwan spent 49 days in

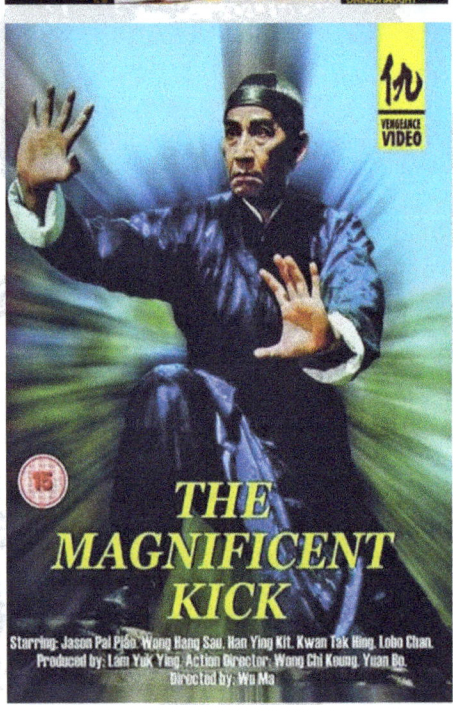

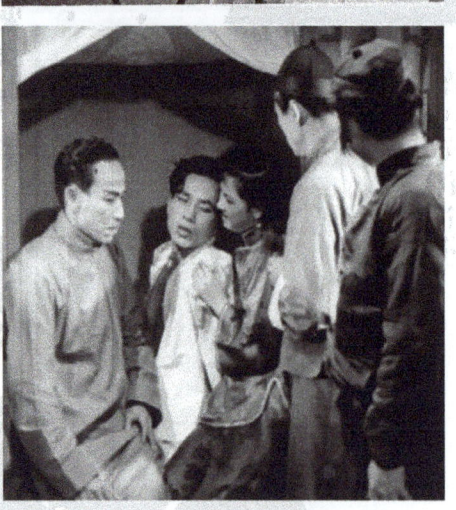

mourning. Moreover, he abstained from any physical contact with his wife for seven years – four longer than the accepted practice.

"The Chinese believe both sons and daughters should obey their parents," he said. "Just look at the crow. Once the baby crow has feathers, he begins feeding the parents. Its the law of nature. My wife understood my devotion to my mother," Kwan said, his eyes looking at the floor.

Despite Kwan's success as an actor, he felt that only what he termed "Chinese traditionalists" knew his name and accomplishments. "In America, kids are raised with American history," he noted.

"Therefore, there wasn't much of a chance to impress or imprint on them what I was saying."

Its a pity, really. Real-life heroes don't come around that often anymore.

About the Author: Dave Cater is the Editor-in-Chief of Inside Kung-Fu magazine.

JAY LEE RECOMMENDS

"I like Wong Fei Hung – The Conqueror of the Sam Hong Gang. Its one of the last ones, from 1969, although it looks like it was shot in the 40's, as the series barely progressed production-wise in twenty years. But several gags and bits from this were borrowed in late kung-fu films, such as Lau Kar-Leung's Heroes of the East (1978)."

A filmography of over a hundred films and even more TV shows can be a bit intimidating! If you're wanting to dive into the Kwan Tak-Hing movie-verse, here are six films to start with, gentle reader! After that, its up to you....

Aces Go Places IV (1986) – AKA Mad Mission 4: You Never Die Twice – Directed by Ringo Lam - In truth, its not much more than a cameo, but a really good one, and (drumroll!) co-starring Shih Kien!

Dreadnaught (1981) – Directed by Yuen Woo-Ping – Co-starring Yuen Biao!

The Magnificent Butcher (1979) – Also Directed by Yuen Woo-Ping - Co-starring Yuen Biao and also Sammo Hung!

The Skyhawk (1974) – Directed by Chang-Hwa Jeong

Wong Fei Hung's Battle With The Gorilla (1960) – Directed by Wu Pang - C.mon! Do you actually need anything else besides the title, there? (If so, check out the movie poster in the accompanying photo!)

The Whip That Smacks the Candle (1949) – Directed by Peng Hu – Kwan Tak-Hing's first time onscreen as Wong Fei Hung!

CHANIMATION
The Cartoon World of Jackie Chan
By Thorsten Boose

The New York Times, in its article "Jackie Chan, American Action Hero?" from its January 21, 1996, issue writes the following about the now world-renowned superstar: "In person, Chan is an irrepressible performer, punctuating his anecdotes with comic gestures and exaggerated faces. "The former kung fu clown is declared a comic stunt actor by the New York Timcs. Even though today the multi-million-dollar businessman Chan has a creative empire behind him, he has never lost touch with his inner child. Comics, video games, practical jokes and pranks – the "happy go lucky" actor expresses this both privately and in his movies. And what do (inner) children want most? Play with kiddies the same age. It was only a matter of time before a real-life comic book character like Jackie Chan became a real comic book hero and turned to the young audience. So let's look back at a few examples from Jackie Chan's filmography where not the real one but its 2D or even 3D counterpart amuses kids young and old.

Drunk, Snaky, Crazy Monkey

Admittedly, the first example in particular is not for the target group of up to 13 years of age. Still, it's worth mentioning since it's Jackie Chan's first cartoon appearance, kind of.
In the 1960s and 1970s, the Japanese manga and television series "Lupin III" enjoyed great success thanks to its creator Kazuhiko Katō. The artist, better known under his pseudonym Monkey Punch, caused a stir because his characters and

stories did not correspond to the usual shallow Japanese comic model: the master thief Lupin made a name for himself thanks to explicit depictions of sex and violence.
Actually, exactly the two elements from which a (later) Jackie Chan always distanced himself. But by the late '70s, Jackie had finally broken box office records in East Asia with his hit trio "Snake In The Eagle's Shadow" and "Drunken Master" (both from 1978) as well as "The Fearless Hyena" (1979). The Japanese distributor TOEI became aware of the movies and asked artist Monkey Punch to create three motifs in the then current design trend.
It didn't stop there. For the third film, "The Fearless Hyena" (1979), a drawn intro was produced especially for the Japanese market in the style of "Lupin III". It's meant to be reminiscent of the characters from "Lupin III", Daisuke Jigen and Fujiko Mine, and in Jackie Chan-style, as the New York Times would put it, with comical gestures and exaggerated faces opening the film – with a drawn Jackie, which hardly resembles the original.
Did Monkey Punch and TOEI subsequently lay the foundation with their "monkey marketing" that years later Jackie got the voice of the monkey in the "Kung Fu Panda" series?!

Before the adventures...

"City Hunter" (1993) is similar to "Lupin III". However, the opening credits feature drawings of Ryo Saeba, the manga character that Jackie brings to life in the Wong Jing film adaptation in a silly but

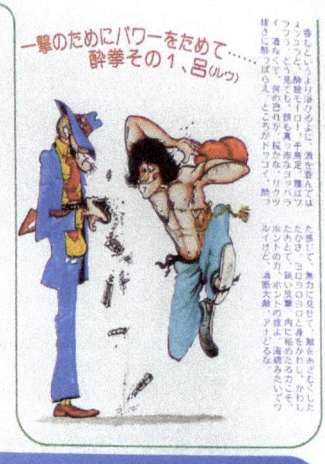   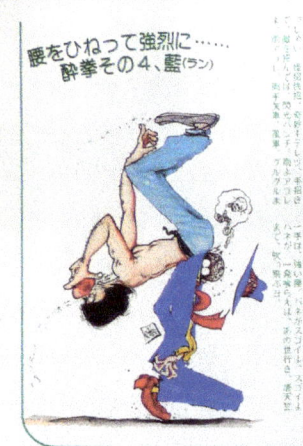

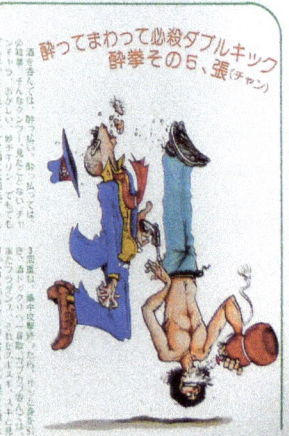 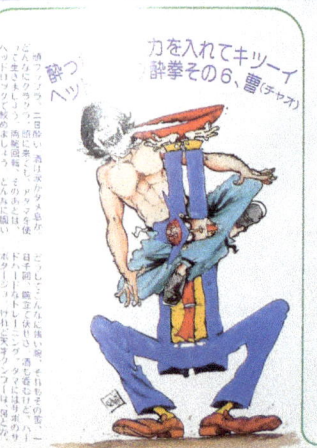  

somehow timeless way.
There are umpteen examples from the animated pop culture over the decades in which Jackie Chan has guest-starred as a 2D or 3D version of himself (though he didn't voice most of them). For example, in the brutally funny MTV series "Celebrity Deathmatch", in which a Jackie Chan made of clay – clearly recognizable this time – competes against an animated JCVD. Referee is Chuck Norris.
Jackie Chan also takes on one of the most famous Japanese children's series called "Shin Chan". In a 2000s special, the famous clock tower stunt from "Project A" (1983) is re-enacted by a well-hit cartoon Jackie after a minor scuffle at a bar involving Yuen Biao and Sammo Hung.

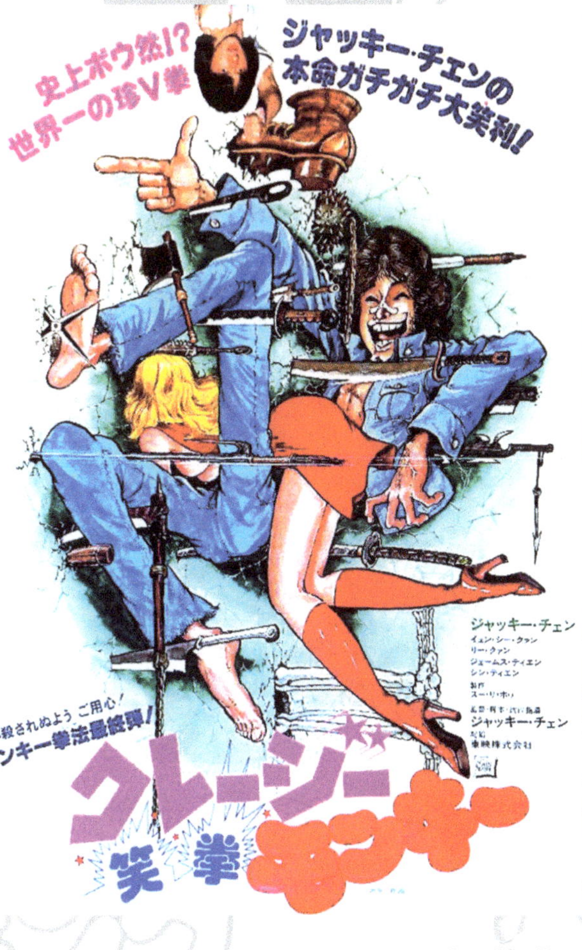
史上ボウ然!?
世界一の珍V拳
ジャッキー・チェンの
本命ガチガチ大笑利!
ジャッキー・チェン
イェン・シー・クァン
リー・クァン
ジェームス・ティエン
シン・ティエン
ジャッキー・チェン
東映株式会社
笑い殺されぬよう ご用心!
モンキー拳法最終弾!
クレージー
笑拳
モンキー

スネーキー
蛇拳
モンキー

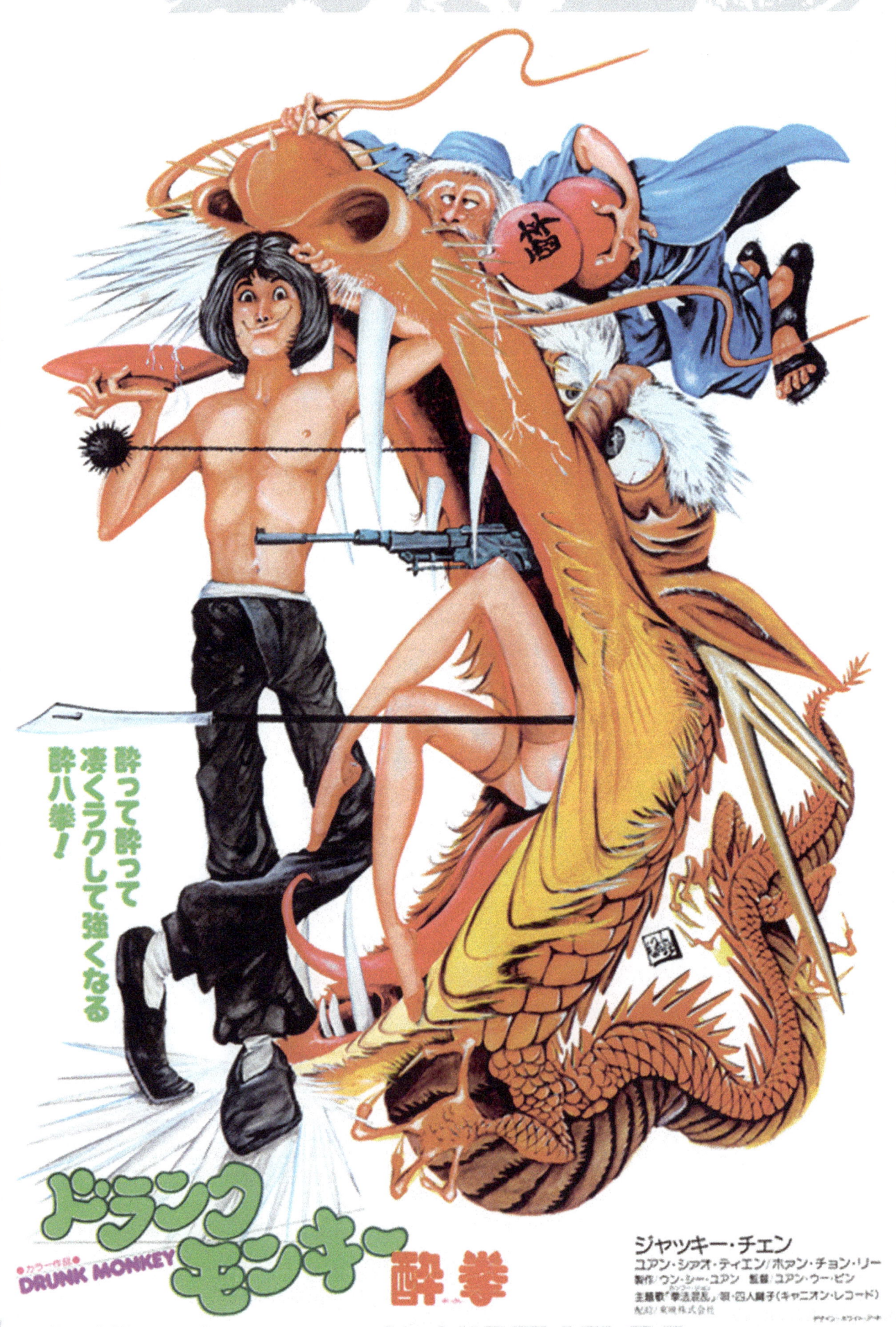

These cartoon homages to the king of stunts are only briefly mentioned. Because they show that even before Jackie's own efforts in the new millennium to turn himself into a cartoon character, other producers saw the potential in doing so. But Jackie wouldn't be Jackie if he didn't have a big adventure in mind.

Jackie Chan Adventures

The millennium got off to an extremely successful start for Jackie Chan thanks to "Shanghai Noon" (2000). In September of the same year, the action comedy legend ended up on US television. JC Group partnered with Sony Pictures (Columbia TriStar Television) to develop the "Jackie Chan Adventures" animated series. Although Jackie didn't dub himself, he appeared in real life in every episode. In five seasons with a total of 95 episodes, kids enjoyed the latest adventures of 2D Jackie every Saturday morning. It was not uncommon for the trained viewer to recognize a few gags, stunts or entire scenes: The JC Group used their boss's cinematic repertoire and turned the main character somehow into Asian Hawk from "Armour Of God" (1986).

What is special about the children's series, in addition to the many references to Jackie's own films, is that at the end of each episode, Big Brother himself answers a question asked by a child about his work, life and Chinese culture.

As is often the case with US TV series, "Jackie Chan Adventures" milked the marketing cow until not a drop was left. Books, comics, VHS and DVD releases, toys and figurines, trading cards and two video games followed.

Unfortunately, fans are still waiting for an official release of the entire series to this day (picture shows a well done bootleg box). The Chinese were faster with Jackie's second television series. But before we're going there we are heading towards Taiwan and Hong Kong.

The Miluku project

Taiwanese filmmaker Edward Yang recognized the technical potential of computer graphics in the early 2000s. He founded the company Miluku Technology & Entertainment. Miluku would go on to produce large-scale animated films and series. The first attempts were made primarily online with animated clips based on Adobe Flash technology.

In 2002, the JC Group entered into a cooperation with Edward Yang's Miluku, which envisaged several animated projects. As a test phase, there was a Flash animation on the Miluku website with Jackie Chan drawn in four small roles:
1. playing the piano and doing somersaults and kicks,
2. a Marlon Brando in "The God Brother" where Jackie stuffs his cheeks with dim sum and smears oil in his hair,
3. Jackie as Rhett in "Gone With the Wind" as well as

4.Jackie as Bogart in "Casablanca". For a long time, Jackie's Hong Kong office had the cardboard figures from the planned TV series, which was already being discussed in 2004 together with an animated film, including an almost life-size 2D Willie Chan. Unfortunately, the little Miluku clips aren't found on any releases of Edward Yang's films in home cinema format (also less thematically appropriate), but maybe that will change soon... From the Miluku web project with Jackie Chan, the plan to produce a full-length feature film using Edward Yang's animation technique was quickly hatched. Yang introduced Chan to this during the success of "Jackie Chan Adventures". The advantage of Yang's technique: principal photography could have been faster. It is rumoured that the production of "The Wind", Miluku's first planned animation work, started back in 2004 with many investors, an investment of 200 million Taiwan dollars, and should conquer the Asian market with a planned theatrical release in 2007. Edward Yang passed away from colon cancer in June 2007, so "The Wind" remains an unfinished film by him and Jackie Chan to this day.

The Wind concept art

But maybe that will change soon. Articles online have been reporting for a number of years now that Chinese production company Enlight Pictures has taken on the unfinished work and is said to have resumed work on it. The new title "Chasing The Wind" is supposed to be a tribute to Edward Yang.
As to how much of Yang's vision will show up in the film, if it even shows up at all, and how much of the original Miluku Jackie would be left... let's take a deep breath.

On the nose

Before we move on to the next big animated series by and with Jackie

Chan, episode 109 of the Japanese anime "Gintama" has to be mentioned at this point. In the episode aired in June 2008, the hero wants to infiltrate an extremist party called the "Anti-Foreigner Faction" and has to pass a test. A running gag is Jackie Chan's big nose. Jackie's performance in "City Hunter" as Ryo Saeba also gets mocked.

But in the last test, the hero is supposed to be accompanied by Captain Dragon, who, of course, just happens to look like Jackie Chan from "Project A" (1983). The title of the last test: Project Z, under the modified theme song of "Project A". As with "Shin Chan", the famous clock tower stunt is recreated here and mixed with elements

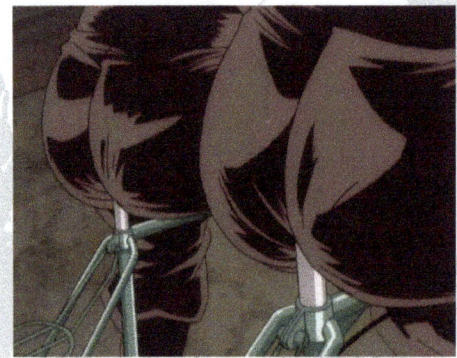 

from "Shanghai Knights" (2003) and "Rob-B-Hood" (2006).

The icing on the cake is served when an animated Sammo Hung (as Fatgo here) appears in an "Enter The Fat Dragon" style. Even Yuen Biao is made fun of – a firework of gags for every fan of the Three Brothers.

Jackie Chan's Fantasia

Fantasy has been demonstrated by the many cartoon artists from all over the world up to this point. But what Chan the Man himself delivered now should build on the successes of "Jackie Chan Adventures" economically and artistically. It is questionable whether this has been achieved.

Jackie Chan, anime artist Huang Yu-Lang, also known as Tony Wong, and those in charge of Nanjing Hongying Animation Entertainment got together early on to plan Jackie's first Chinese TV animation series in 52 episodes of 12 minutes each. Again, 2D Jackie becomes an adventurer, similar to Asian Hawk in "Armour Of God" (1986), and must survive adventures with the help of his human, animal, and mechanical friends.

The premiere took place during the 5th China International Cartoon and Animation Festival on April 29, 2009; the interest was great at first. The aim of the animated series was to bring China's cultural heritage to a young audience through Jackie Chan's fame. Similar to "Jackie Chan Adventures", only for a younger audience up to ten years. Jackie Chan said via video message at the 2009 press conference: "I hope that my animated series will give children a happy and meaningful experience."

Although an English language version was produced in Hong Kong by Red Angel Media for All Rights Entertainment and appears to have premiered on Disney Channel Asia in 2011, it is still awaiting an international release or broadcast in the West. Luckily, fans can at least get the series home in the original language from countless variants – DVD and VCD.

For those interested in the entire series, its background, an episode guide in three languages, and all home theatre media that has been released, I have written a detailed article called "Jackie Chan's Fantasia: Will the forgotten anime series from China be running in Germany soon?" in my Jackie-Chan blog (https://bit.ly/JCFantasia).

The concept of letting the real Jackie Chan have his say personally at the end of each episode was also consistently implemented here. Just like marketing with comic books, figures, DVD and VCD releases and much more. By the way, the real Jackie also appears on screen for split seconds during each episode, so watch carefully!

Little Big Spin-Off

The Chinese 3D production "The Adventures Of Jinbao" (2012) is actually the first real 3D animated Jackie Chan movie. It's about an ancient warrior who is catapulted into another dimension by magic and transformed into a panda who is supposed to break a curse. One way or another, in any case, two successful films were combined here.

The reference to "Kung Fu Panda" (2008) is unmistakable. But Jackie's award-winning "Little Big Soldier" from 2010 is also picked up here; the film is sort of a spin-off, and Jackie is said to have officially given the production company permission for his animated likeness. Here, we also directly recognize the "chanimated" 3D-Jackie. He even took over the dubbing for the Cantonese version. Rob Schneider did the job for him for the English version entitled "The Adventures Of Panda Warrior".

All New Jackie Chan Adventures

All good things come in threes, thought Jackie Chan when he went public with his third animated series in 2017. And again it's about adventures. In "All New Jackie Chan Adventures" a young audience between five and twelve years is addressed. The fantastic adventures of Jackie and his dream team, who are supposed to protect children from nightmares, are told in two seasons of 52 episodes each. The 3D animation series, also known by the alias "J-Team", was produced by the Chinese company Khorgas JJ Culture Media Co. When the series was announced, it was said that a feature film was planned for 2019. So, they wanted to make the newly founded animation company economically viable. But who is behind "Khorgas JJ Culture Media Co., Ltd."? I reveal that information and much more about "All New Jackie Chan Adventures" in my online article "All New Jackie Chan Adventures: Episode Guide for the Chinese animated series" (https://bit.ly/AllNewJCA).

Jackie Chan relocated his business headquarters to Beijing and Shanghai after leaving Hong Kong around 2009. Therefore, the choice of founding a new film company in this rather remote part of China is surprising, but can be explained by the fact that one might wanted to try to strengthen exactly this emerging region. The region around Xinjiang has been of interest to investors such as Coca Cola, Volkswagen, Siemens and BASF for several years.

Business information for "Khorgas JJ Culture Media Co., Ltd." suggests a founding date of July 26, 2016, in the same city. Co-founder and legal representative is none other than Wu Gang. Wu Gang has been part of the Jackie Chan stunt team (5th generation) since the 1990s and is still loyal to his boss to this day (see my online article "Jackie Chan's stunt team members from 1976 to today in a complete overview").
As with "Jackie Chan Adventures" (2000-2005) and "Jackie Chan's Fantasia" (2009), "All New Jackie Chan Adventures" aka "J-Team" produced many promotional merchandise products, as well as four exclusive comic books. Jackie makes a personal appearance again this time both in the intro of the series and at the end of

each individual episode ("Jackie's Tips"). When the actual planned animated film will appear in cinemas can generally be questioned. Because since then, a successful Sony collaboration has been started with "Wish Dragon" (2021), which under certain circumstances can result in a franchise – for the "All New Jackie Chan Adventures", the target group may even be missing today.
But who knows what else Chan the Man has planned for his "chanimated" future. Perhaps he will take up Edward Yang's original idea of Miluku and also produce small web series. Or the "Spartan X" comic series is experiencing a revival. After all, according to Renée Witterstaetter, a cartoon show and much more was already being planned back then in the 1990s.

Thanks to Fabian Schweitzer for his "Jackie Chan Adventures" DVD box set photos.

RATINGS KUNGFUSION

ALAN DONKIN AND PETER SCOTT TAKE A LIGHT-HEARTED LOOK AT THEIR OWN BESPOKE KUNG FU MOVIE REVIEW RATING SYSTEM

Think back to the time you watched your first kung fu movie. For me, it was probably in about 2007 or 2008. Then, a dam burst, and the trickle became a flood. Soon, I was watching several films a week. After a handful, they started to merge into a single blob of half-memories and fuzzy opinions. Duel of the Seven Tigers? That was great. Ten Tigers of Shaolin? That had a fantastic ending. Assault of Final Rival? Erm… Something to do with hair? The area of my personality that craves order started to flex its muscles. My oldest friend, Peter, with whom I watched the films, felt the same. With this in mind, he came up with a solution. It quickly evolved into a review system that we still use to this day. I had a chat with him about how our system evolved, its strengths and its weaknesses, and whether or not we'd change anything about it.

AD: I seem to remember that the system we developed for keeping a record of movies, and our thoughts about them, happened very quickly. We decided on the format within about fifteen minutes.

PS: That's not entirely true. At first, we didn't bother to split the score ratings into categories.

AD: Ah, ok. So we just rated the films out of ten?

PS: Yes. You suggested rating them out of five, but I said it wasn't precise enough.

AD: Some of the areas of the 'pocket' review haven't changed at all. Next to the title we included the source of the print.

PS: That's in case we found a different print source. We could look back and see if we'd already seen it.

AD: That's right – people were putting out a lot of customs back then. Jamal Tairov was sourcing new prints.
PS: We also included a brief cast list and a selection of notable scenes. Those were snippets designed to trigger the memory.

Category					
Kung fu quality	~40	38	35	30	20
Dubbing/subtitles	~10	8	7	6	7
Soundtrack and music	~10	8	9	8	8
Story quality	~20	18	15	15	14
Quirkiness/Originality	~10	8	8	8	8
Casting	~10	9	8	9	7
		89	82	76	64

AD: I remember being a few beers to the good by this point on most evenings, so I couldn't be bothered to put in much effort. That soon changed as I got more anal about details.

PS: Well, 'anal' is an anagram of your name.

AD: Excellent. Well done. I see we put a little summary comment in brackets, too.

PS: It wasn't long after these initial reviews that I decided that it wasn't thorough enough. I hit upon the idea of a rating system out of 100.

AD: I recall a few lively debates about the weighting of different categories?
PS: Yes. I think we tweaked it several times, then ran a few tests.

AD: 'Kung fu quality' was the first of the six categories. That had to command the bulk of the score.

PS: Obviously – we were reviewing kung fu movies! We settled on a score out of 40 marks, which is just less than half.

AD: The other larger category was story quality. That was graded out of 20.

PS: The final four were worth 10 marks each. Dubbing/subtitles, soundtrack/music, casting, and quirkiness/originality.

AD: That gave a grand total of 100. After totting up the marks, we rounded it to a mark out of 10.

PS: 81 out of 100 would be an 8 out of 10. 84 out of 100 would be 8 and a half out of 10.

AD: 79 out of 100 would also be 8 out

of 10. So what's the point in rounding? The precision offered by the mark out of 100 proves that the 81 rated film is better than the 79 rated film.

PS: Calm down, Vorderman. It's just a simple summary. You don't have to get your knickers in a twist over two marks.

AD: This was your system! Aiming for greater precision! Do you think we made any errors with this system?

PS: It's not flawless. No system is perfect. But the areas of assessment are weighted well.

AD: Are they, though? What about 'quirkiness/originality?' Is that always a good thing?

PS: If they make the effort to make the movie fresh and unique, it should be recognised. Think of Drunken Dragon (1985). That was insane. We both loved that.

AD: Agreed, but then consider Firefist of the Incredible Dragon (1982). That was quirky, with its floating heart and things. It was also completely and utterly awful.

PS: I liked it.

AD: You would. It's a horrendous film and it shouldn't get extra points for being weird. I feel that our category for 'quirkiness' doesn't distinguish between 'weird good' and 'weird bad'. We maybe should have reduced it to five marks, or dispensed with it entirely.

PS: No, I don't agree. It's definitely worth celebrating when it works. The times it doesn't are few and far between.

AD: The 'kung fu quality' category is solid. It's two fifths of the final total. If anything, we could have increased that to 50 marks.

PS: Is that kung fu from a technical standpoint? Or are we talking about exhilaration?

AD: Both. Technically good kung fu skills and choreography can be excellent to watch.

PS: It can also lack excitement. Plus, how do you decide what's technically good or bad?

AD: I know what you mean. Undercranking can result in some absurd sights. I loved the action in Five Fighters from Shaolin (1984), but some people don't like undercranking as a filming technique at all.

PS: Some of the most exciting, visceral fights to watch are raw and untidy. I've always liked the end of The Magnificent Chivalry (1971) where Wang Yu is trying to defeat an opponent in the mud. It's hardly a showcase for slick martial arts skills. It's messy and brutal.

AD: Exactly. And we haven't even got into the complications of styles. Should shapes be rated more highly than basher styles? Swordplay more highly than stick-fighting? There's a definite shift in choreography in the mid-1970s. We both prefer shapes – does that mean that the flailing arms of basher choreography should be marked down?

PS: No, otherwise you risk putting a 'sell by date' on certain styles. There's some amazing work in earlier films of the classic old school era.

AD: I guess 'kung fu quality' covers all aspects of choreography, skills and excitement. I suppose it boils down to how much you enjoyed it by the end of the film. The more we pick apart our system, the more fragile it becomes.

PS: What about the other areas? 'Casting' is strong. A good cast can really make a film, and a mediocre cast can really drag it down.

AD: I don't have any complaints with that!

PS: Soundtrack/music and dubbing/subtitles are technical aspects of the film. They're pretty straightforward.

AD: They are. I would offer one caveat.

PS: Dubbing?

AD: Dubbing. It's hardly the fault of the original film if the dubbing is dross. A good dub can elevate a film. A bad dub is excruciating.

PS: What about an amusing dub?

AD: Oh, come on, man! How many whiny 'comedy' voices can you tolerate in a movie!

PS: Subtitles aren't that different. Badly-translated burnt-in subtitles can be horrendous.

AD: Absolutely correct. It ruined Witty Hand, Witty Sword (1978) for me. I didn't have a clue what the hell was going on.
PS: And custom subtitles with poor spelling and grammar…?

AD: They boil my piss. Should this even be a category at all? Too much is left to chance in post-production, the hands of distributors, and botched custom jobs.

PS: Yes. It's not perfect, but again, quality efforts that improve the film, and MAKE IT UNDERSTANDABLE (rather than having to work out what's happening in Mandarin, which is the alternative), should be rewarded.

AD: Fair enough. Let's talk about the review system overall. Does it work?

PS: Of course it works. Sure, tweaks could be made. But it differentiates between good films, bad films, and average films. Even down to a single mark. If you list all the highest marks, they are the films that we enjoyed the most. Therefore, it works.

AD: I have issues with it.

PS: Quelle surprise.

AD: The lowest rating we've ever given was 6 and a half out of 10 for that dreadful Firefist rubbish. That's surely in the 'good' bracket? Five out of ten is average. That means every film in the review book is way above average!
PS: It's just a simplification. Don't get hung up on how 1-3 is bad, 4-6 is average, etcetera. Anyway, you went back and re-graded it.

AD: I know, but it was still a six! You know how much it annoys me to have a numerical system that doesn't make sense!

PS: It does make sense. The bad films get the worst scores.

AD: A worst score shouldn't be six out of ten. What's the point of a rating system where over half of the marks are unattainable?

PS: It's just the way the categories work. Without them, you'd just pick a random score befitting the overall rating.

AD: So I could have given it two out of ten? Well that sounds far more accurate!

PS: Then you wouldn't have the luxury of breaking the film down into different areas. It's highly unlikely that a film's 'soundtrack' would get one out of ten. Or the 'casting' two. Therefore, a lot of the marks are built up in areas that at least provide some merit. That's reflected in the overall mark.

AD: Don't get me wrong, I like the scoring system! It appeals to my youthful love of Top Trumps. However, it's a system that's flawed.

PS: It has flaws. But some of them are only 'flaws' in the sense that they challenge your need for absolute fairness and accuracy. In reality, it's a system that rates the movies we watch in an efficient way.

AD: It's true that all ratings systems have issues. Rick and Toby's Essential Guide

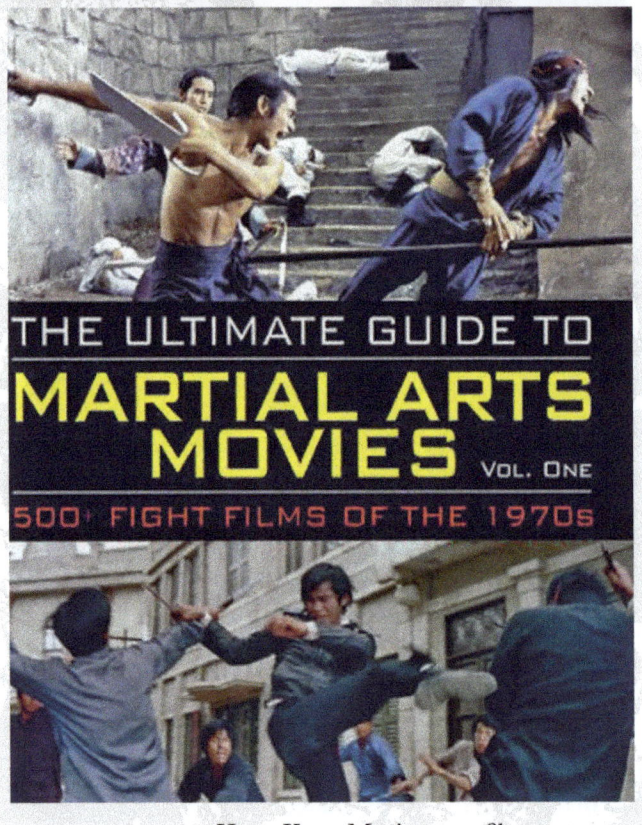

to Hong Kong Movies rates films out of five. It's elegant, it's simple, yet it's restrictive. Every single film lumped into one of five ratings? With no scope for greater precision? Some four-star movies will be far better than others. How do you

distinguish between them? Also, what's the rating based on? A particularly good story? Choreography?
PS: We give twenty marks for story quality.

AD: We do. And it's arguably ridiculous. Would you rather have an average, run of the mill story with killer martial arts action, or a wonderfully-complex, multi-layered story with average action?

PS: I'll slap you in a minute.

AD: I agree that a good story can elevate a kung fu movie, but should it define an entire fifth of its overall rating?

PS: The fallibility of reviewing methods isn't unique to our method, you know!

AD: I know. Dr. Craig D. Reid's The Ultimate Guide to Martial Arts Movies of the 1970s doesn't bother with a final rating. You have to read the text to discover his opinions.

PS: I've got that book. There's a number at the end of each review. It's the percentage of the film that features martial arts.

AD: It's an interesting and unique statistic to include. It doesn't have a bearing on his overall thoughts on the film, though. A film can have loads of poor martial arts to acquire a 42.83 percentage, whereas another movie might embody the 'less is more' ethos and have 21.35% of the runtime dedicated to amazing fight scenes. I know which one I'd rather watch.

PS: Basically, no numerical rating system is without fault. I enjoy the one we use.

AD: I do, too. Far more than desperately trying to note down all the 'notable scenes' in the rest of the review before they fade out of my memory as the credits roll.

PS: It's still a pointless exercise for you. You can't remember them even when they're written down in your own handwriting.

After much grumbling, that's where our chat ended. Readership of Eastern Heroes, what do you think? Truth be told, our review system isn't much of a review system. It's an aide-memoire, combined with a numerical rating that attempts to break down areas of the film into weighted categories. Categories that we recognise are flawed and open to interpretation. However, it's something we enjoy doing, and it's become part of our film nights. Peter has even typed them all up for posterity.

Do you have a review/rating system for watching kung fu movies? Or do you just prefer to watch them and not bother with such a chew on? Perhaps the more technical you make a review system, the more problems it presents. Admittedly, ours is rather complex, whereas Jared King's boils down to 'Good', 'Ok' and 'Bad'.

I'm pretty sure that most of you are shaking your head and saying, 'Just watch the damn film!' I take my hat off to you – once you fall down this rabbit hole, it's bloody hard to get out!

Jackie Chan at the PRINCE CHARLES CINEMA

By Ron Ivey

A rare visit to London for Jackie in 2014. This was the most recent event for JC in England, there was a planned 2018 book signing for his book Never Grow Up, which was cancelled.

A little bit about the PCC:

"We are The Prince Charles Cinema, the last of the independents still operating in London's cine-famous 'West End'. The site itself sprang to life as a Theatre back in 1962 before making the rather interesting shift to becoming a film-house of ill repute, which just so happened to host the UK's longest theatrical runs of both Emmanuelle & Caligula! Then in 1991, the early seeds of The Prince Charles Cinema were planted and from there this mighty little cinebehemoth began to grow. We now find ourselves as one of the most popular Independent Cinemas in the UK (if not THE WORLD!)."

The first film I watched at the PCC was Lady Snowblood with my good friend Ossie, a few of us from my Facebook group (London East Asian Film & Events) went to see Big Trouble In Little China 70mm at the PCC. Amongst my various nights at the PCC there was also a Terracotta Film Club night for Johnnie To's Election, I've been to many a screening at this venue, and various film clubs and festivals screen there.

Myself and Rick Baker (Eastern Heroes) went to the PCC as part of a day out a while back. We first went to the The Making Of Chinatown exhibition at China Exchange, about the history of Chinatown. Then from Chinatown on to watch Enter The Dragon uncut 35mm, at that screening I spotted the director of the Raid films Gareth Evans! Gareth was kind enough to chat about films and I pitched the Kung Fu Cafe to him as he'd be a great guest, and I got a photo with him and Lee Charles outside the PCC. Gareth had watched the film before going to a Gangs Of London meeting. There

is a funny story attached to this random meeting, but it's a tale for another day. More recently a bunch of us went to a preview 4K screening of Everything Everywhere All At Once. If you like a mix of films, the Prince Charles Cinema is for you, also check out London's Genesis cinema.

Tickets for this Q&A event sold out in minutes. I had two tickets and started to receive offers for the second ticket immediately. I didn't

want to sell a ticket (I was offered £100+) and if I gave a ticket away I would please one friend and upset many others, I chose to take my daughter who would enjoy the film and a night out with dad. This was the first night of two, a second night followed, hosted this time by Jonathon Ross at a different venue.

Outside the cinema, I witnessed a bloke wandering down the queue asking about spare tickets for this sold out event, and he got one, at the face value price!

Whilst I was waiting at the bar area I heard a member of security comment on never having seen so

many security teams for one guest. They weren't needed, the audience was well behaved throughout.

The film being screened was Chinese Zodiac, to celebrate the UK release of Jackie Chan's Chinese Zodiac on DVD/Blu-ray, because of which we got this awesome Q&A and film screening. I had not seen the film, and to watch it at a Jackie guest appearance night was chantastic! But let's face it, fans were there for Jackie, people who had never been to the Prince Charles Cinema were desperate to get into this very small gathering to see their idol.

There were signs all over saying 'No Photographs', as soon as JC walked on

stage half the audience took a photo, and some started filming. The room got noisy with shouts and applause as he walked on stage, a real nice vibe, the PCC was filled with very happy fans that night.

A few of us had the opportunity to ask JC a question, I had a question ready which I then ditched! I had wanted to ask if he would ever do a proper bad guy role, something which pushed him as an actor and was a complete contrast to his good guy roles. Unfortunately during the Q&A JC touched on his family films, and not wanting to play the bad guy.

So I fell back on the old fan favourite of asking Jackie if he would do another film with Sammo Hung and Yuen Biao. JC spoke to me for a minute and even ended with saying "Meals On Wheels 2". My daughter filmed this on her ipod, low quality but a nice clip to remember a great night. We can dream, but it seemed like a nice answer to something we will never see.

There are always some people hanging around outside events for autographs, I did see some fans waiting to catch JC as he left.

The owner of Pimp Shuei (a kung fu

film themed basement bar), wanted me to ask JC if he had heard of Pimp Shuei. Haha, I wasn't about to do that, but I did switch my shirt for a Pimp Shuei t-shirt to highlight the bar.

Everyone wanted to be at this night or in some way connected to it. I'm glad I attended, and myself and my daughter had a memorable evening.

Here is some audience footage from the night by Ben Lewis: https:// youtu.be/ Wre96xFTWWo

Check out Ben's other videos for two videos from the BFI Q&A Jackie night, and some JC fan videos.

"In honour of the DVD and Blu-ray release of Chinese Zodiac, Jackie Chan took part in a special screening and Q&A at London's very own Prince Charles Cinema. The evening which featured the legendary martial artist talking about his love of pandas, his U.S. breakthrough and who he'd most like to work with next. Also, he sang, quite a lot." Empire Magazine

All in all, a very special night and still the best Q&A I have ever been to.

See you out there!

JUGANDO CON FUEGO INTERVIEW

With Robert Samuels

Asking what makes this film successful is like asking what the warmest log on the fire is. Jugando con Fuego is slick action-thriller that is written and directed by Nicholas Ortiz. With a runtime of approximately 37 minutes, this is a short sharp rollercoaster which is not easily forgettable.

This is a classic revenge story about a CIA agent, James Forge. Having to step down into retirement, his past hasn't finished with him and it gets personal. Left for dead, Forge wages a one-man war to finally end it once and for all. The film is told in current time with flashbacks, creating a film that unfolds the storyline to the viewer, when necessary.

The film stars Robert Samuels as James Forge. Robert worked in Hong Kong during the prime of 1990's Hong Kong cinema; working with Jackie Chan, Sammo Hung and Yuen Woo-Ping to name a few. Robert showcases his acting ability and screen presence here, creating a performance that would appeal to large mainstream audiences and not just fight fans.

The martial art scenes in the film are outstanding; showcasing Chinese kung fu, MMA, Judo, bladed weapons, gun-fu, with a brief gore scene; that really puts the icing on the cake. The fight scenes are well choreographed with sharp camera angles showing the true potential for the film and it's creators.

The beauty of short films is it has given great directors such Richard Linklater, Harmony Korine and Kevin Smith a platform to showcase their talent and progress further. It is rare to see a production of this quality and substance within a short, so I hope this film and it's crew go far. I would like to see the full potential of this film with further backstory and the build-up to Forge's ultimate confrontation.

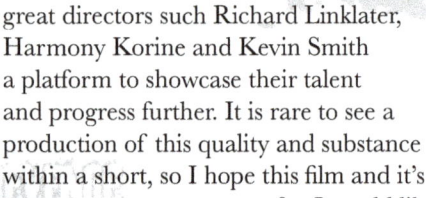

I can't predict the future but I think it's safe to say this won't be the last time we hear about Nicholas Ortiz or Robert Samuels…….

As a good friend of Eastern Heroes magazine, The Man himself, Robert Samuels, has agreed to talk about Jugando con Fuego with us.

SP: Firstly, congratulations on the film and thank you for talking with us. How did this film come about and how did you get involved?

RS: My partner Robert Jefferson and I discussed the idea of doing a film in the vein of Denzel Washington's "Man on Fire". We talked about some ideas but it wasn't until we spoke to Orlando Candelario, who has worked with us many times. Orlando recommended we should link up with Nicholas Ortiz who he's worked with on many occasions, to

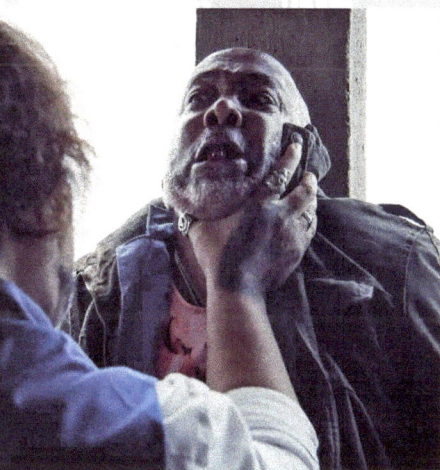

see if this is something we could all join forces on.

I had seen Nick's previous film "Black Beauty" and I was very impressed with his style as a director. We had many meetings and Nick liked our concept. He asked if he could write the script and we said yes! There was a certain sense of trust that had to be given in order for this work. The final script blew us away. We all signed off and pre-production began.

The goal was to tell a story and present a unique visual style to wow the audiences. This would be my first film as a lead actor and not co-star. I wanted to show that I could carry a film as the lead protagonist....but I'll let the audience make that decision.

SP: The film has a lot of good reviews, nominations for awards and the momentum is building; what are the plans for the future? Are there plans for this film to be revisited or is there something new on the cards?

RS: We were blown away at the responses from the festivals across the world. Short films don't usually make a tremendous amount of noise because of the nature of how those films are marketed and it's a difficult sell with the big distributors. However, we do plan to release the film sometime in May 2022 for the audiences around the world.

It will be released with a bonus short called "Behind the Bullets". We want the audience to not only see the film but to experience the adventure of shooting an international production.

In addition, we will use the film to show potential investors that the big screen version of this film is a great addition to the slate of films coming in the next year; with an original concept, great action, and characters the audience can root for.

SP: The fight scenes seem to have an ode to different eras and disciplines of martial arts. The first fight is quite traditional then to the bathroom scene which was more modern. How was it training with the Action Director, Orlando Candelario? Did you have much influence in the fight sequences?

RS: Yeah we didn't want to create Hong Kong style action per-se. We wanted to make sure the action compliments the story. So Orlando Candelario & Hector Soria took their time to make sure each action sequence had its own narrative feel.

We didn't have a ton of time to preview the action so we made sure to map out each action scene to compliment the story. Most of the heavy action builds in the third act to make sure the audience takes a rollercoaster ride to the end of the film.

There is an action team, ran by Angel Brophy in Tijuana, called "B-Squad Action Design". Angel and his team came on board to help us with creating the action. All the action motifs have their own feel and nothing is the same from scene to scene.

SP: The "making of" documentary is very well edited and reminiscent of 90's street films with the fisheye

lens, time lapse, decent music etc. which I love; was the film as easy to make as it seems or did you face any issues?

RS: Yeah so the plan was to create a special featurette to accompany the film as we realized that the film is just under a 40 minute run time but we also wanted to have a bonus for the audiences to show how this journey occurred. We plan on releasing the "Behind the Bullets" special along with the film which combined will give audiences around 75 minutes of content.

The film was easy to make because of the amount of time pre-production took. We spent five months, planning, planning, and planning! We had to because we were not only shooting in the United States but in Mexico as well.

Special thanks to the Santi Brothers and our U.S based Executive Producers Mark Wiley & Tayari Casel whom supported us at every turn in the production.

SP: What are your best memories about making this film?

RS: For me the best moment about this film was having a team and a director that understands how to create visual images to capture the audience's attention. The people of Tijuana, Mexico are simply amazing people. The love and support we experienced cannot be put into words. Plus the local producers in Mexico made sure we had everything to pull off the film. We are forever grateful.

SP: Is there anything else you would like to add?

RS: We want to thank everyone that helped us achieve this film. Special thanks to Simon Pritchard and Rick Baker and the entire staff at Eastern Heroes Magazine.

SP: Thank you for taking the time to talk with us and we wish you all the best in the future.

SPOTLIGHT ON
Aiodhan M Cochrane

"Martial arts for me was a way in helping me deal with my anxieties"
"Bruce Lee also made a quote to explain this.
"When I look around, I always learn something and that is to be always yourself, and to express yourself. To have faith in yourself, do not go out and look for a successful personality and duplicate it…. Start from the very root of your being, which is How can I be me?.

It is easy to talk about how you broke your arm but not so easy to talk about a broken mind. When we are feeling anxious or fearful we can find our safety in repression in other words hold it all in for fear of judgement. Martial arts for me were a way in helping me deal with my anxieties. The book Zen in the Martial Arts by Joe Hyams describes this perfectly.

" A dojo (practice hall) is a miniature cosmos where we make contact with ourselves – our fears, anxieties, reactions and habits. It is an arena of confined conflict where we confront an opponent who is not an opponent but rather a partner engaged in helping us understand ourselves more fully".

Upon recovery from alcohol and drug addiction it took much time to stand on my own feet due to the physical disorders from my abuse. 10 months later after rehab, I went to Manila in the Philippines to learn the art of Kalis Ilustrusimo which is a bladed based art founded by Tatang Antonio Ilustrismo and teacher was Mang Romy Macapagal. The familiar journey of martial arts is to learn skills at a high level and become teachers but this was not my path even though teaching is my profession I had no desire to open a school. However, I began to question why have I travelled thousands of miles to learn an art that I could achieve with jus a bus ride. Then while on a break a lightbulb went off in my head and that's when the idea came to travel the world competing in different weapon formats but using the principles that I learned. I was 49 years old at this time and as a result of my self-identified maturity that this was not about winning trophies or medals but to assist with enhancing my skills to break the habits of whats coming next and to deal with unexpected attacks also, it was an opportunity to face my anxieties as opposed to avoiding them. But my self identification of maturity would prove futile at Cold steel.

No my first experience or tournament fighting was the Cold Steel Challenge in Ventura California and I approached this with high expectations. In preparation, I would drill everything that I learned

Page: 47 Eastern Heroes Issue #5

and would spar regularly with my senior brother in Ilustrisimo Richard McMahon. By nature I was a bull in a China shops stampeding through whatever stands in my way. I believed by developing speed and strength I could bulldoze my way through at the Cold Steel Tournament. Leading up to this challenge my ego began to overtake my rational thinking and I began to have romantic feelings of actually winning the tournament and what it would mean. So here was me like Caine out of the Kung Fu series travelling alone like a wanderer who was going to dazzle everyone with my swordsmanship, however the desire to win became so great that the night before I would twist and turn like a coiling python shedding his skin with tension and anxiety. When the day came of the tournament I may have wandered in like the wandering monk but I walked out like a beach front donkey wearing a straw hat because I got schooled. My mind was fuzz whilst my opponent was calm and rational picking me off with perfect defensive responses every time I went in to attack. Where were all the techniques and skills that I practiced because they were not available to me because I was so obsessed with practicing everything I failed to cultivate what I had learned? It would be the last time I would let ego overtake my aim and for this to work I had to completely liberate myself from the obsession of winning and stick to the original plan which was to learn. The dialogue from Bruce lee in Longstreet summed this up perfectly.

Like everyone else, you want to learn the way to win, but never to accept the way to lose, to accept defeat, to learn to die is to be liberated from it. So when tomorrow comes, you must free your ambitious mind, and learn the art of dying."

This was to change my whole approach, when training I would not only learn but cultivate my skills. Richard was very patient and paid attention to detail so I could understand how to strategise. I developed a rational mindset through the understanding of distance, timing and measure and over a period of time I improved.

The anxious mind means we are rigid and vulnerable to snapping which meant as part of my recovery I had to confront my anxieties as I spent many years in avoidance through drinking. When I was under the influence I would become the social chameleon and adopt a character that I felt suitable depending who I was socialising with. I have seen this in Martial Arts students when they adopt personality traits of their teacher. Bruce Lee also made a quote to explain this.

" When I look around, I always learn something and that is to be always yourself. And to express yourself. To have faith in yourself. Do not go out and look for a successful personality and duplicate it…. Start from the very root of your being, which is "How can I be me?" Anxiousness is a part of life and it is needed as part of our survival when faced with a dangerous situation. However, it can sometimes get out of control followed by responses such as 'I must fight this, I will take this on, I will face this. When we adopt this approach it means we are are separating ourselves and seeing the disorder as a detachment in which may fuel anxiety. From the new edition of the Tao of Jeet Kune Do there is a quote that's describes a more appropriate response.

" Let yourself go with the disease, with it,

keep company with it- this is the way to be rid of of it."

Acceptance is the tool here which cleared the fog of distortion and I was able to focus on mind and body working together. It was not long before I began to see the results of my transformation in 2015 I registered for the World Wide Historical European Martial Arts Championship. I was informed by the organisers that I should try some HEMA lessons since I my background was Filipino Martial Arts. In addition, I was also told I could never win the special award of fighter of the day. I was on fire about this one and looked forward to the opportunity and felt good about it. My weapon of choice was the Dussack sword which is a Czech cleaver hunting sword and its length was similar to what I was used too. The weekend of fights just flowed and the plan to cultivate worked as I took my first world title since being sober with a weapon I had never seen before. Also, I was voted fighter of the tournament from that division. I went on to raise money for different charitable causes for every tournament I entered involving stick, spear, sickle, Chinese Jian, backsword and knife. The medals are a bonus but the real winning is the opportunity to face my adversities as opposed to avoiding them and to bring balance to my mental state.

SCARLETT CROSS
The Battle from Script to Screen!
By Dean Meadows

If there was ever a definitive example of not giving up on your dreams and doing what you love, it could possibly be me! For seventeen years, I've been determined to establish myself as a scriptwriter and filmmaker, and for seventeen years it seems there has been one obstacle after another trying to knock me back. However, like Rocky Balboa once said, "it's not about how hard you hit, it's about how hard you can get hit and keep moving forward", and

that brings us to 2022 and 'Scarlett Cross: Agents Of D.E.A.T.H.' being chosen as official selection at the 10th Anniversary of The Urban Action Showcase and Expo – International Action Film Festival, alongside its premiere distribution via streaming platform, Troma Now, which for me is the culmination of seventeen years of perseverance and just not taking no for an answer in this business.

As I sit here writing this article, it's hard to believe that despite all the beatdowns, the blood, sweat and tears, and the professional and personal problems that many of the cast and crew have faced along the way, this grindhouse era inspired labour of love, which took seven years itself to make, finally arrives on the big screen in the original home of the grindhouse, 42nd Street and Times Square, thanks to Demetrius Angelo and the team at UASE.

Whilst I had been dabbling in the independent film industry since 2005, the first full script I wrote was called 'Friday's Child' back in 2010, sadly that project never saw the light of day thanks to an executive producer who was full of promises but eventually delivered nothing, most importantly the financing that was required for a project and cast of that size. At the time, Queen of Martial Arts movies, Cynthia Rothrock, 80's music legend and actor Adam Ant,

Film and Television star Michael Brandon, and 'Machete' himself, Danny Trejo were all attached to the project. Thus, feeling very disheartened, I locked myself away and kept writing, developing another four scripts, 'Blood Rush', 'Bitchfight' and 'Ghost Warriors', (two further potential collaborations with Cynthia,) and the original 'short' version of 'Scarlett Cross'. I borrowed equipment, assembled crew,

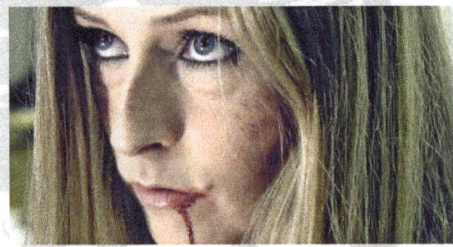

and shot a couple of promos for 'Blood Rush' and 'Bitchfight'. The idea was to keep shooting whatever possible, in the form of promos or trailers, until one way or another I could finally get one of my projects financed. That opportunity

came in the form of 'Scarlett Cross' after teaming up with lead actress and Associate Producer, Kat Clatworthy and Executive Producer, Laurence Owen who gave the project the green light and, 'Scarlett Cross: Agents Of D.E.A.T.H.' became the first movie to go into full production.

I've always been a huge fan of 'old-school' exploitation movies, so there are several genres and sub-genres from the grindhouse era that have influenced 'Scarlett Cross', both in the writing and shooting of the film, from Japanese, Hong Kong, Filipino and American Martial Arts movies, to 1970's and 80's Euro-Horror and Italian Crime flicks with just a pinch of British Gangster capers thrown in for good measure.

Female assassins, killer nuns, mad monks, ninjas, zombie super soldiers and a whole bunch of violence, bad language and nudity, not necessarily in that order all make an appearance during the 90-minute running time! Make no mistake this is definitely not aimed at a PG audience and I'm hoping that 'Scarlett' will establish a brand for the production company Pentagram Pictures, giving the viewer a glimpse of what to expect from future

productions which are currently in development or pre-production.

We have some amazing martial artists and upcoming British talent involved with this movie, Tayah Kansik is a lethal weapon and looks deadly on screen in her role

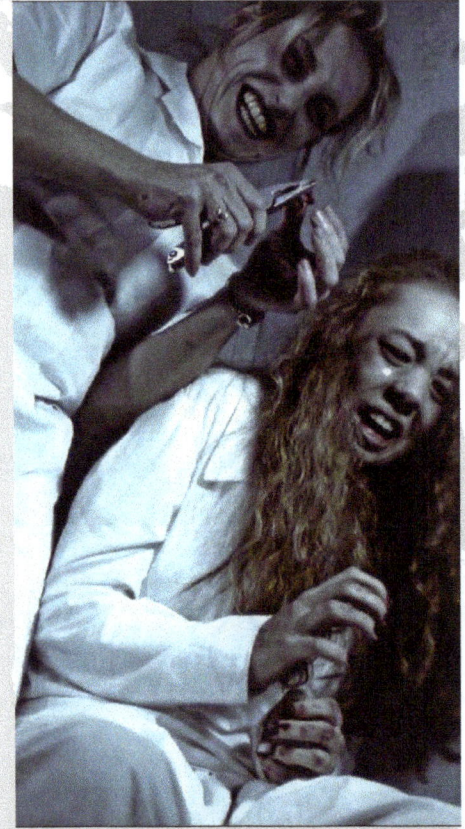

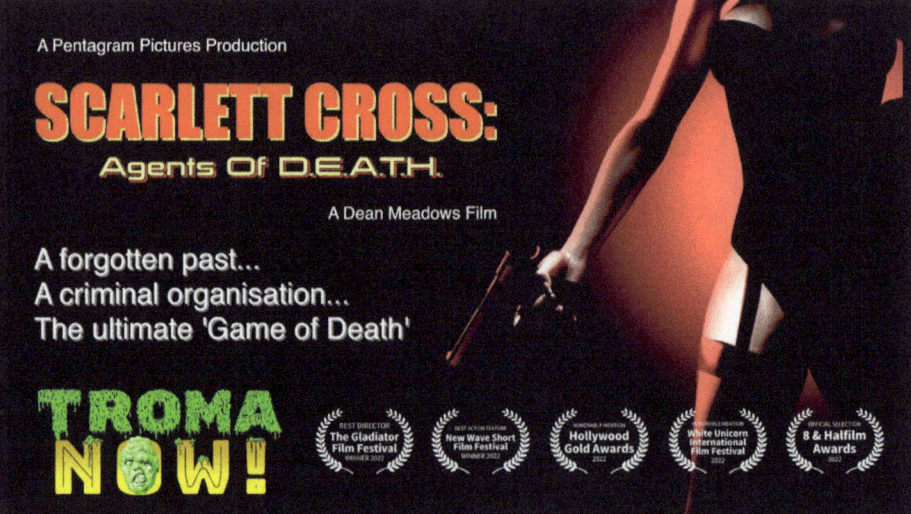

as 'The Bodyguard', Hannah Farmer as 'The Yakuza' is also one to watch, Maria Lee Metheringham sets the screen ablaze as 'The Assassin' and Sky Rose is perfect in her villainous role as 'Reaper'. You certainly won't be disappointed if you're a fan of femme fatales or the fighting females genre.

The martial arts sequences in 'Scarlett Cross: Agents Of D.E.A.T.H.' are choreographed by Karate and Kickboxing Champion, Dean Williams, who has worked with everyone from Steven Seagal to Benedict Cumberbatch. I grew up watching Hong Kong movies, but I really didn't want that style of action for all the choreography in 'Scarlett' as I felt at the time there were enough filmmakers doing that kind of thing and I wanted to do something completely different. That said, there is a little nod to Bruce Lee and the 'Bruceploitation' genre in the most unlikely scenario, alongside the classic Ninja films from the 1980's. Aside from that the movie is hard hitting and gritty, influenced as much from the violence of modern action and horror as it is from the 'old-school' martial arts and exploitation era that defines it.

But let's not forget where the original inspiration for this film came from. At six years old I discovered Bruce Lee thanks to 'Enter The Dragon' and the wonderful world of VHS videocassettes, I discovered Bruce Li, Sonny Chiba, Jackie Chan, Wang Yu, Chuck Norris and Joe Lewis about a week later and then there was no turning back, I was completely hooked on the Kung-fu and Martial Arts movie genre as a kid. This obsession for cult cinema would further develop in my formative years with a love of exploitation films from directors such as Roger Corman and Cirio H. Santiago, alongside my passion for Cannon films, European horror movies, and the work of Japanese filmmaking legend Akira Kurosawa. With this eclectic melting pot of inspiration in mind, I wanted 'Scarlett Cross: Agents Of D.E.A.T.H.', to ultimately become recognised as a cult movie of the modern age. Therefore, having the longest running independent film studio and cult legends, Troma Entertainment recognise the work and initially pick up the film for distribution on their streaming platform 'Troma Now' was a huge compliment to myself and everyone who has believed in, or worked on the project throughout the last seven years to finally bring this grindhouse inspired action exploitation movie to the screen. Rest assured, this is only the beginning…

If you're in the New York area, 'Scarlett Cross: Agents of D.E.A.T.H.' will be screening at the AMC Empire 25 Cinema as official selection on 5th November 2022 at the Urban Action Showcase and Expo International Action Film Festival. The movie is also available now to stream via Troma Now! The first month of Troma Now is free and can be found at the following link: https://watch.troma.com/ and on most streaming devices such as Amazon FireTV, AppleTV, AndroidTV and Roku.

For further information on 'Scarlett Cross' and future productions visit www.pentagrampictures.co.uk and catch up on social media at www.facebook.com/deanmeadowsfilm

A BRUCE LEE PILGRIMAGE

By Michael Nesbitt

The name Pam Hadden was synonymous with Bruce Lee during the 1970s and early 1980s. Like most of the early Bruce Lee fans, Pam had fallen in love with Bruce when his movies were released in the UK back in the early 1970s, and by 1976 she had teamed up with the monthly poster magazine, Kung Fu Monthly, to start off the second Bruce Lee UK Fan Club, after the first fan club dissolved. Pam, along with her friend Carmella Rapa released the first Bruce Lee Secret Society newsletter in September 1976. However, with the help of their regular column in Kung Fu Monthly, the fan club become so popular, that Camilla decided to leave, as it was taking up too much of her spare time. This meant that Pam would run the fan club herself until it folded in early 1984. Pam's love for Bruce, went above and beyond that of a normal person, her dedication to the fan club was evident to all of the members, and she would become friends with quite a few of them. In 1979, Pam was given an opportunity of a lifetime, to visit the Hong Kong homeland of Bruce Lee. The trip became one of the highlights of Pam's life, and somewhat of a pilgrimage.

Since Pam discovered Bruce Lee way back in 1973, she had always dreamed of visiting Hong Kong, a place which held a lot of intrigue and mystery for all Bruce Lee fans. In 1975 both Kung Fu Monthly and Rhona McVay's Bruce Lee Fan Club had advertised trips to Hong Kong, but this trip was different, this trip was Pam's own personal adventure to try and learn more about the biggest Kung Fu star that had ever lived.

Pam was working for British Airways at the time, and with her discounted ticket, she set off for Heathrow Airport on Thursday the 9th of August 1979. Pam's trip didn't start off too well, as the plane was grounded for four hours in Frankfurt Germany because of engine trouble. Back in the 1970s, there were

(Pam Hadden ©Tony Lundberg 1980)

David Chan & Russell Cawthorne (Photo ©Pam Hadden 1979)

very few direct flights to Hong Kong from London, and Pam's plane had to stop at Bahrain, Bombay and Bangkok before finally touching down at the now long-gone Kai Tak Airport in Hong Kong. An emotional Pam was one of the first passengers off the plane, and she couldn't hide her excitement. As she later stated in an interview: "I was on the verge of tears, it was a very emotional time for me." For her trip to Hong Kong, Pam had decided to stay at the YMCA/Peninsula Hotel on Waterloo Road in Kowloon. She had specifically chosen that area, because of its significance to Bruce Lee. Nathan Road, where Bruce Lee grew up, was not far away, and she spent many hours just strolling around the streets, taking in the exquisite sights, sounds and people.

Just like my very own personal journey to Hong Kong in 2001, she was disappointed at first not to see anything relating to Bruce Lee in the shops, buildings, and museums. I think most people imagine Hong Kong being the Bruce Lee hub of the world, but in reality, it took them many years to celebrate the success of its most famous star. A disappointed Pam spent the next few days in search of anything Bruce Lee-related, and it wasn't until Wednesday the 15th of August that things started to look up. Having already made arrangements in advance through the offices of Golden Harvest in London, Pam was granted a visit to the now famous Hong Kong Golden Harvest Studios. Robert Burton, the Vice President of distribution at Golden Harvest, met Pam at the Peninsula Hotel for lunch, where they chatted about Bruce Lee and Hong Kong in general. At the time, Burton had worked for Golden Harvest for over two and a half years but had been living in Hong Kong for 15 years. After finishing

Pam found herself alone, when Burton was called to the telephone. She was given the privilege to explore the studios herself. She couldn't quite believe that she was now following in the footsteps of her hero, and once again things became overwhelming for her.

A few hours later, Pam return to the main building, where she was briefly introduced to Raymond Chow, the head of Golden Harvest and Bruce Lee's business partner. Betty Kwong, Raymond's secretary, then introduced Pam to a lovely young man called Jackie Chan. Back in 1979, Jackie wasn't as famous as he is today, and Pam would later state that Jackie resembled an almost Chinese-looking Charles Bronson figure. After meeting back up with Robert Burton, they toured the main building, and Pam was even shown Bruce Lee's old dressing room, which unfortunately was locked, due to the occupier now being used by Golden Harvest's biggest movie star Jackie Chan. Pam was then introduced to the director of international advertising and public relations, Russell Cawthorn, of course, Pam went on to explain to both Russell and Robert, about Kung Fu Monthly and her Bruce Lee Society Fan Club, both seemed interested and were willing to help her in any way they could.

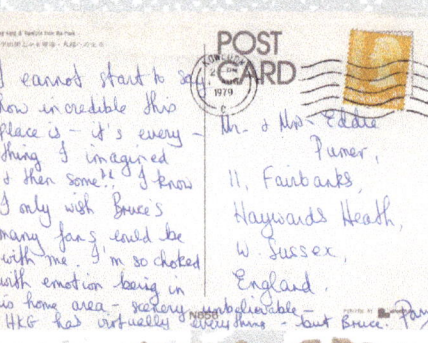

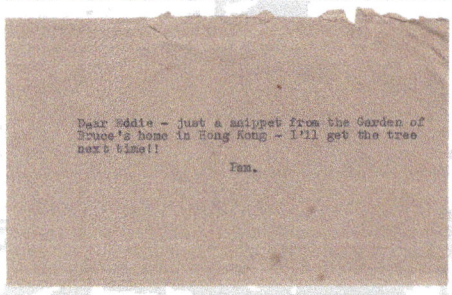

their meal, Burton escorted Pam to the Golden Harvest Movie Studios, and once they were through the large cast iron gates, Burton began showing Pam around the studio lots. At one point during the tour,

On Thursday, the 16th of August, a reporter, Ken McKenzie, interviewed Pam for the Hong Kong Standard Newspaper. Pam had generally disliked reporters, mainly because of the many lies they

had written about Bruce Lee in the past. However, she found Ken to be a big fan of Bruce Lee's and he was very interested in Bruce's popularity back in the UK and had given a very favourable write-up in the newspaper. Having now run the UK fan club for several years, one of the Hong Kong supporters met up with Pam

Robert Lee Photo ©Pam Hadden 1979)

in the following days, to show her around important sites relating to Bruce. Among the first destinations she visited, were the Queen Elizabeth Hospital, where Bruce Lee had passed away, the Happy Valley Cemetery, which was shown in Enter the Dragon, and Betty Ting Pei's apartment. Her final destination was Bruce Lee's old home at 41 Cumberland Road, a place which she wasn't looking forward to visiting, as she had heard that it was now a house of ill repute. Once again the emotions overtook her, and as she approached the entrance, she asked the man standing at the gateway if it was okay for her to take a few photos of the garden and house. He surprisingly said yes, and she strolled around the garden entrance taking photographs. At one point she took a few leaves off one of the bushes in the garden, a keepsake for her and a few of her closest friends back home in the UK. As Pam was driven away from Bruce's old home, she couldn't help but think about what Bruce would have made of his old home being used for such an immoral purpose.

One of Pam's main goals while visiting Hong Kong was to try and track down Bruce Lee's brother, Robert. Up to that point, she had been unsuccessful, but her friend once again came to the rescue. He advised her to contact Betty Young, who was a public relations officer at the Hong Kong TVB Studios. Having followed his advice, Betty had agreed to contact Robert on her behalf, and not long after, she was told that Robert would be phoning her at her hotel within the next hour. Robert phoned as promised, and a meeting was set up for 7:30 pm in the hotel lobby. Robert had been famous in his own right as a singer, but he was probably most famous in Hong Kong for being the brother of Bruce Lee. Once Robert had arrived to meet Pam, she found him to be attractive and very charming. Robert asked Pam about his brother's popularity in England and he was very happy to hear that he had a huge fan base there. The meeting itself didn't last very long; however, Pam managed to ask Robert some questions which he happily answered.

Pam's trip to Hong Kong had been a success, and in the few hours she had left before flying home to London, she posted some postcards off to her family and friends, including one to the singer, radio presenter and Bruce Lee fan Eddy Pumer. She then took the lift to the rooftop of the Sheraton Hotel, where she took in the glorious view of Hong Kong harbour. Once Pam was back home, she reflected on the trip of a lifetime that she had just experienced, and remembered that she still had the leaves that she had taken from the bush in Bruce Lee's Garden. She kept a few for herself, and carefully packaged up what she had left into small plastic pockets, and placed them in an envelope. These she had given out to a few of her closest friends who had helped her throughout her journey while running the Bruce Lee Society. Unfortunately, Pam passed away in 1991, but her memory and love for Bruce Lee will always live on.

URBAN ACTION SHOWCASE & EXPO 10th ANNIVERSARY SPECIAL

By Simon Pritchard

Demetrius Angelo

The UASE is a leading Action Entertainment platform that promotes and celebrates diversity and inclusion within the blockbuster genre. The UASE is celebrating their 10th Anniversary on the 4th and 5th of November 2022.

After working in the movie industry for many years, Demetrius Angelo founded the UASE in 2013. This was due to mainstream cinema's continued resistance to promote multicultural principal characters. This resistance runs deeper, "If you poison a flower after the beauty dies, the poison works down to the roots". So, the opportunities for aspiring filmmakers, producers, actors, etc have been over-proportionally reduced.

The UASE's Diversity in Action initiative enables opportunities to meet, and network with independent and mainstream professionals. Their principal goal is "To restore equal value to imbrued images based on color, creed, and credentials by advocating and promoting heroic content reflecting multicultural images and interest in media".

Each year the UASE host an Expo in Times Square, NY. This runs over two days that offers celebrity panels, seminars, master classes, Cosplay competitions, collectible vendors, and other fan experiences. The Expo also welcomes Urban Pop culture content creators, production, and entertainment companies to showcase their products to the fans.

The Friday night before the main event is The Urban Action Showcase International Action Film Festival and Honoree Awards. This is a red carpet event, hosted by Rochelle Miller and Vanessa Bontea. The UASE honours, past, present, and future, multicultural achievements in action entertainment.

The Urban Action Showcase International Action Film Festival (UASIAFF) is held on at the AMC Empire 25 Theatres in Times Square and ranks in the top two per cent of more than 60,000 film festivals and creative contests worldwide*. The UASIAFF also includes the Warner Media Action Short Film Competition for Live Action Short Films

The UASIAFF offers awards and prizes valued at over $5 million* including funding opportunities, Distribution with platforms such as Amazon Prime, Amazon Instant Video, Amazon Fire TV, Roku, Apple TV, and more, there is so much to do and see there.

We have the pleasure of, and exclusive chats, with the Founder and executive producer, Demetrius Angelo, Red carpet host of UASE, actor, poet, fashion designer, Rochelle Miller, Vanessa Bontea, and Eastern Heroes good friend, martial arts master, actor, director and producer, Robert "Bobby" Samuels.

Thank you for talking with us and we look forward to meeting you all in November.

*Source - https://filmfreeway.com/UrbanActionShowcase

The Founder and Executive Producer - Demetrius Angelo

SP: Thank you, Demetrius, it is an honour speaking to you.

Can you please explain the barriers you endured within the mainstream industry trying to promote multicultural principal characters and how did this make you feel and drive you towards change?

DA: We live in a nation where a few people make decisions for the masses and the challenge is to convince the few of the value of the whole. Life itself has many challenges; all we can do is facing them. As a Martial Artist I try to approach things strategically rather than emotionally I have grown to realize that resistance is necessary for growth.

SP: How did you take your concept

of a platform for multicultural cinema and turn it into a reality?

DA: I had the privilege of being a consultant at HBO for 23 years and had developed many relationships between working at HBO and running my own production company ASC Productions. I took my experiences from producing events at HBO as well as my own events at NY Comic Con and created a blueprint for what we know as the Urban Action Showcase and Expo.

SP: The UASE premiered in 2013, what do you remember about the first Expo and that weekend?

DA: I was overzealous in my efforts to be like my much more experienced predecessors. I scheduled 3 days of events at 3 locations. I recall not sleeping for days trying to get everything set up. I lost everything I had but we make a great first impression and it paid off the following year.

SP: How did Warner Media Action (formally Cinemax) become involved?

DA: I was a consultant at HBO and had access to the executives in order to pitch our UASE proposal. Cinemax is a sister brand to HBO. Warner Media came into existence after AT&T bought Warner Bros in 2018. HBO is a subsidiary of Warner Brothers.

SP: We're also chatting with your good friends, Rochelle Miller, Vanessa Bontea and Robert "Bobby" Samuels, how did you first meet them and how have they supported the UASE over the years?

DA: Vanessa was cast in one of my films back in 2009. She then became a student of mine at my NYC Action Actors Academy where I taught Actors combat for the screen. Rochelle came to me as a host from an independent television show and was set up at our Red Carpet. Ironically Robert Samuels was one of the celebrity guests that Rochelle aka Lachocolate Box was interviewing. Vanessa had always been like family; she is very supportive of our diversity

and inclusion initiative. Rochelle and Bobby have been like family since day one and are very supportive of all of our events both live and virtual.

SP: The progression of the UASE has been phenomenal. From the last ten years, what have been your proudest moments and achievements?

DA: The proudest moments of the UASE have been seeing the success of our Alumni Filmmakers in the industry and the Behind-the-Scenes Production of The Last Dragon 30th Anniversary Blu-Ray. Joseph Le is Alumni Filmmakers who went on to become a part of the Fight Choreography team for Shang Chi with the great Andy Cheng. Mayling Ng is an Actor who co-starred in the award-winning Urban Action Showcase International Action Film Festival film Blood Hunters: Rise of the Hybrids, has gone on to star in Lady Bloodfight and as Mongol in The Suicide Squad

SP: What progression have you seen in multicultural cinema since you founded UASE?

DA: AMC, Netflix, and the CW have done a lot to produce shows with heroic characters of colour. From Black Lightning to Luke Cage and Into the Badlands, the industry has really increased the presence of people of colour in heroic roles but still has a long way to go to balance out the scales. New OTT platforms like Tubi TV are helping push independent content into the mainstream which intern gives us more choices to see ourselves as heroes.

SP: How do you envisage UASE evolving over the next ten years?

DA: I hope to see the UASE expand its audience reach and content creative opportunities for distribution and funding. We started out with distribution on Cinemax, and Amazon and have moved to our own OTT Platform on Roku and Amazon called Urban Action Showcase Cinema Television (UASC TV). It would be great to partner with Netflix or Tubi TV in the near future. Netflix representatives will be present at this year's event on November 4th and 5th.

SP: Do you have any last words for the readers?

DA: Yes, believe in yourself; believe in the power and ability that God has given you to fulfill your destiny and the desires of your heart. Know that it will most likely be an uphill battle, but you will be stronger once you reach the top. Always remain at peace with what you are endeavouring to do as it will take time and patience to meet those mandates. Thank you, Ricky Baker, for this incredible opportunity to tell our story of trial and triumph.

The hosts of UASE - Rochelle Miller and Vanessa Bontea

Rochelle Miller

SP: Thank you Rochelle for speaking with us. When do you first meet Demetruis and how did you get involved with the UASE?

RM: I was initially introduced to Demetrius Angelo at the very first Urban Action Showcase. Although I was booked to cover the UASE Red Carpet by an independent media group, I actually did not get the chance to meet him until the 2nd day of the event. A little over a week later, Demetrius reached out directly, to thank me for covering the Red Carpet he then went on to explain his vision and future plans for the UASE & the International Film Festival.

SP: The UASE premiered in 2013, what do you remember about the first Expo and that weekend?

RM: I remember the initial UASE event in 2013 as being super exciting and recall truly being in awe of the moment! Due to traffic and initially being given an alternate address, I arrived at the event, and then was held at the HBO Bldg - approximately 10 mins after the Red Carpet started. I recall entering the room and was immediately met by an usher who asked if I needed help. As she walked me over to the brightly lit UASE backdrop, someone grabbed my coat and handed me a mic - less than 10 min's later, I was interviewing Michael Jai White! I then went on to interview other influential action film stars, and independent filmmakers, in addition to many other men and women from the stunt community.

As a stage performer, fashion designer, and host/public speaker, the opportunity to Host the UASE was the first of what would become many years of my covering Red Carpet events! That said, although I was new to the task, I also felt it was important to develop my own hosting persona and not mimic anyone that I had seen on air previously. It was at this point that I decided to fuse my love for the stage and fashion, by using my stage name "La Chocolate Box" (defined as "the

sweetly pretty, overly sentimental one") as part of that Red Carpet personality. In addition to complimenting attendees on their red carpet "looks" my Hosting voice was found by relating my love of martial arts and action movies to those whom I interviewed!

SP: The progression of the UASE has been phenomenal. From the last ten years, what have been your best moments and achievements?

RM: Over the past 9 years, I have been privy to so many incredible Hosting moments with the UASE, there are almost too many to list! That said, there are a few that do indeed stand out! I once interviewed Kelly Hu (I believe this was in 2013 at the very first UASE), and was fan girling on her appearance as "Lady Deathstrike" in Marvel's "X2: X-Men United". Immediately following the interview and while still on the red carpet, she leans in and says to me – that was one of the best interviews she's ever had. Needless to say, with my being so green in this part of the entertainment industry, I was unbelievably grateful for this accolade.

Other moments that I will never forget are those that made me tear up or cry. This was keenly apparent when conducting a dual interview with Ron Van Clief & Michael Jai White immediately following UASE's Mantle of the Dragon ceremony in 2019 whereas Grand Master Ron Van Clief handed over the title of "Black Dragon" to Grand Master Michael Jai White. Love, respect, unity, and comradely were abundant in those moments following and I was feeling all the feels!

Another historical interview was with "Lu Feng" / 'The Centipede' (via his interpreter), for the 40th Anniversary of "The Five Deadly Venoms". During this quiet and low-key interview, I totally lost it just by looking into Mr. Feng's eyes. It was such an incredible feeling to know that very few fans of the Shaw Brothers film work have ever had the opportunity to meet their martial arts idols – and here I was 40 years in the making, meeting one of mine! Nevertheless, surreal was an understatement! That said, although it did cross my mind that Mr. Feng may have seen my antics as a bit off-beat or a little over the top – this did not stop me from being a teary-eyed mess for the entirety of the interview.

A couple of weeks later I received a call from Demetrius advising he watched the footage of my interview with Lu Feng. Before he could say a word, and while laughing at myself I immediately began to apologise for getting so emotional, stating further that I hoped it didn't reflect badly on UASE. He immediately told me not to! He admitted that until this moment, he did not realize how much of a fan I was of martial arts. He then asked what am I thinking of, which moved me so much during this particular interview. I went on to tell him that growing up, I was the only one of 5 children (with many nearby cousins), who truly appreciated martial arts films and that at times I was teased mercilessly because of it! However, it made me stronger to pretend I was a 'karate' expert and to this day, I still maintain an impressive old-school martial arts collection!

SP: You have met many stars on the red carpet. Who has been your favorites any why?

RM: Throughout the years, the people that some may consider "stars" became more like family to me!

• Oso Tayari Casel is my "day one" because I met him before working on half of the UASE.
• Cynthia Rothrock, her story of women's empowerment in the action film industry is powerful.
• Taimak, there is more to him than meets the eye. Michael Jai White has a keen eye and a great sense of humor.
• Fred "The Hammer" Williamson, spoke with my mother by phone because I told him she was a huge fan.
• R. Marcos Taylor is truly down to earth and not afraid of transparency.
• Robert "Bobby" Samuels, is a cool dude, wears the hell out of a suit, and has pushed thru & conquered race barriers overseas.
• Cary-Hiroyuki Tagawa loves music and can dance!
• Stu Bennett aka "Wade Barrett" stood 16 or more inches above me with my wearing 5-inch stilettos!
• Demetrius "Oaktree" Edwards, has a great smile and made me laugh during our interview.
• Ron Van Clief is a super sweetheart and a very sharp dresser.
• Gloria Hendry, because a few years before I had the opportunity to meet her virtually she came out to a UASE event and stood by the Red Carpet area smiling at me for quite some time. When went to introduce myself to her afterward, she told me that I was doing a great job and to keep making us look good!
• Nafessa Williams is a true beauty and totally down to earth.
• Vincent Lyn, because he wears chucks with his suits!
• Ric Myers is super informational and is a very convincing Santa during the holiday season.

If I missed anyone, blame my head not my heart! ...Because I Love You ALL!

SP: How do you feel that multicultural protagonists, have progressed within the mainstream within USA cinema since UASE started?

RM: Honestly, I feel that there are still not enough main character/ action film rolls being offered and/or being made available to persons of colour or to women In my opinion, part of the UASE's mission was to not only share what made many of the diverse multi-cultural films so good back then but as well show a new generation of filmmakers that there are other ways to acknowledge, create and prosper in that area of entertainment. But there are still challenges and thus a ton of work is still left to do! I once wrote a poem called "Back to Black Action" on behalf of the UASE, which included the following passages:

"Let's bring it back to basics! Break it down, and make the industry transform. Bring back diversity in film, bring it to the forefront, and take it by firestorm.

Do it again! Support the rising action film genre, now on an upward ascent. Let's do it again! Let's bring the back-to-black cinema out of early retirement.

Let's keep doing it! Keep demanding a return of the urban hero, and movie classics, Let's do it right now! Let's take the cultural controls out of big Hollywood's 'we pick the hit movies', baskets"

SP: How do you envisage UASE evolving over the next ten years?

RM: My hope is that the UASE will continue growing internationally and that more people will see the need for people of different backgrounds and skin tones in varying movie roles. If the recent controversy over the casting of Halle Bailey as "The Little Mermaid" didn't open our eyes to start these much-needed conversations on diversity in films, then I'm not sure what will. I also hope that eventually the UASE itself will be celebrated as the catalyst as that conversation starter, somewhere down the line.

SP: Do you have any last words for the readers?

RM: I would remind those who are paying attention: the UASE's quest for "Diversity" does not mean change forever, it doesn't mean all or only black action films, or does it mean that any one group is better than another. It simply means that since this world / the USA is occupied by people of differing cultural backgrounds, why not have those backgrounds represented in the movies that we all pay to see? Accepting the need for diversity concept itself is much like understanding the major differences in a chicken noodle soup vs. a hearty stew. Unlike the stew, the broth of the soup is thin, contains one meat (only 1 demographic represented in a film), and usually, two vegetables (produced/directed by one or two well-known companies). As such, the chicken noodle soup lacks the stew's flavour because the stew is fashioned from many vegetables (multi-cultured, multi-diverse cast) cooked, often with different proteins obtained from many areas (from different demographics) that are simmered simultaneously (they work together), and whose smooth texture is derived from the ever so often stirring of a pot (those who bring attention to a need for change in this area).

That's it! Problem solved: We need more pot stirrers and hearty stew like the UASE, because there are too many chicken soup lovers in the world!

Venessa Bontea

SP: Thank you Vanessa for speaking with us. When do you first meet Demetrius and how did you get involved with the UASE?

VB: Thank you for having me. I first met Demetrius sometime in 2012 when I auditioned for one of his film projects. I was given a small role and I really enjoyed my day on-set working together. Demetrius ended up reaching out to me for something else after but said it involves some training and martial arts, on-screen film fighting training, and asked if I was interested that answer was an emphatic, "hell yeah!"

SP: The UASE premiered in 2013, what do you remember about the first Expo and that weekend?

VB: Wow.. I remember thinking how come there isn't another festival like this in the world?? then being super glad and really proud that it was Demetrius who brought it to life. He's the perfect person for that. I remember being nervous but excited and really wanting to do a good job on the red carpet. I'd be interviewing some great, iconic actors, people, and martial artists and wanted to make sure they felt comfortable on the red carpet answering questions and also had a good experience with that as well.

SP: The progression of the UASE has been phenomenal. From the last ten years, what have been your best moments and achievements?

VB: My best moments have been meeting all the incredible people, actors, filmmakers, stunt men and women, and fans that have attended the festival and who support Demetrius and our projects. I've met some incredible souls and have fostered some great friendships through the festival. Right before the pandemic, I had the honour of having 2 projects I was on screen at UASE in the same year. The first one is called "Catfight" that I'm very proud of and the other was a short, fight scene I did with Demetrius that he choreographed and we trained for a few months. We also shot it at the most beautiful beach location on Long Island.

SP: You have met many stars on the red carpet. Who has been your favourites any why?

VB: Oh man, it has always been a star-studded affair! I can't pick a favourite because they're all amazing! Bobby Samuels, Juju Chan, Jenel Stevens, and Michael Jai White… just to name a few, but I am a wrestling fan and did not expect to ever see one of the WWE superstars on this red carpet so I totally geeked out one year when I got to interview Stu Bennett. He premiered a film that year at the festival called "I am Vengeance." That was a fun surprise that year.

SP: How do you feel that those multicultural protagonists have progressed within the mainstream within USA cinema since UASE started?

VB: I think there have been some strides and openings made for more multicultural representation overall in the industry and US cinema but to lead an action film here, you still need to be an A-list movie star most times. I love UASE because you can see the progress, representation, and future upfront. It welcomes everyone and their films, not just the projects that have a lot of funding or movie stars. There are so many different

filmmakers, martial artists, and films that have come through this festival that showcase the heartbeat of what's really happening in the other levels of cinema.

SP: How do you envisage UASE evolving over the next ten years?

VB: Demetrius is always elevating and leaning into new approaches to UASE! It gets better every year. I see it growing into a bigger festival and what he's doing now with VR and Augmented Reality is really interesting.

SP: Do you have any last words for the readers?

VB: I hope the readers can support and come to the festival if they're in New York City or join us online at the UASE Metaverse!

Action star, Director, Producer, and Martial Artist - Robert Samuels

Robert "Bobby" Samuels

SP: Thank you Bobby for speaking with us. When do you first meet Demetrius and how did you get involved with the UASE?

RS: I first met Demetrius Angelo right before the launch of the 1st Annual Urban Action Showcase. A friend of mine said he was looking to recognize and celebrate Black Action Stars of yesterday and today. When I spoke to him and he shared with me his vision for the event I couldn't say no! I've gone to many events over the years but none quite like Urban Action Showcase. At first, I came just as a guest to receive an Award for my work in Hong Kong Cinema. Then as the years continued I played a more active role in supporting Demetrius and his Vision. Every year the event has grown and more Industry Filmmakers now support this triple-A-rated event.

SP: The UASE premiered in 2013, what do you remember about the first Expo and that weekend?

RS: I remember so many Iconic Legends of Action Cinema being in the house. The atmosphere was palpable with everyone supporting the HBO / Cinemax brand. I remember so many talented new filmmakers having their films entered into competitions and the joy of the audiences supporting their films.

SP: The progression of the UASE has been phenomenal. From the last ten years, what have been your best moments and achievements?

RS: For me, I never really realized how much of an impact my film career in Hong Kong and in the U.S has had on so many fans of the Action genre. I have received so many distinguished Awards that I am truly humbled to have been recognized for example, "The Hong Kong

Legends Award", the first recipient of the Jim Kelly Lifetime Achievement Award just to name a few.

SP: How do you feel that that multicultural production has progressed within the mainstream since UASE started?

RS: I think now since the inception of Urban Action Showcase. People are

paying attention to the historic film work that people of color have contributed to the action genre. Thanks, to Demetrius Angelo, for having a vision of inclusiveness and recognizing heroes that reflect our image celebrating the past, present and the future. I can't only imagine the next milestone in 10 years.

SP: How do you feel that that the multicultural protagonists have progressed within mainstream cinema within the USA since UASE started?

RS: I think the Multicultural protagonists are here to stay. 2023 can only show growth for people of colour in the film industry. I plan to continue to reflect that value in all my future films. Especially, from a Director's point of view.

SP: How do you envisage UASE evolving over the next ten years?

RS: I know over the next ten years so many exciting and interesting things will be happening and I plan to be along for every year. It's definitely a way for me to pay it forward to the next generation of Action Stars both male and female. So I look forward and challenge all of my peers to contribute in some way to the next generation.

SP: Do you have any last words for the readers?

RS: Yes, I would like to personally thank all the supporters that have gotten us to this point .special thank you to Demetrius Angelo for creating an event that can clearly be labelled as the only one of its kind. Special thanks also to Eastern Heroes magazine for taking the time to recognize the contributions so many have given over the years.

R4 FILMS

From R4 FILMS and the Executive Producers Robert "Bobby" Samuels and Robert Jefferson, comes exclusive reviews on Jugando con Fuego, Shadow Fist 1 & 2, and interviews with Robert "Bobby" Samuels.

Jugando con Fuego

Jugando con Fuego (2022) is a slick action-thriller that is written and directed by Nicholas Ortiz. With a runtime of approximately 37 minutes, this is a short sharp rollercoaster that is not easily forgettable.

This is a classic revenge story about a CIA agent, James Forge (Robert Samuels). Having to step down into retirement, his past hasn't finished with him and it gets personal. Left for dead, Forge wages a one-man war to finally end it once and for all. The film is told in the current time with flashbacks, creating a film that unfolds the storyline to the viewer, with all twists and turns, when necessary.

The martial art scenes in the film are outstanding; showcasing Chinese kung fu,

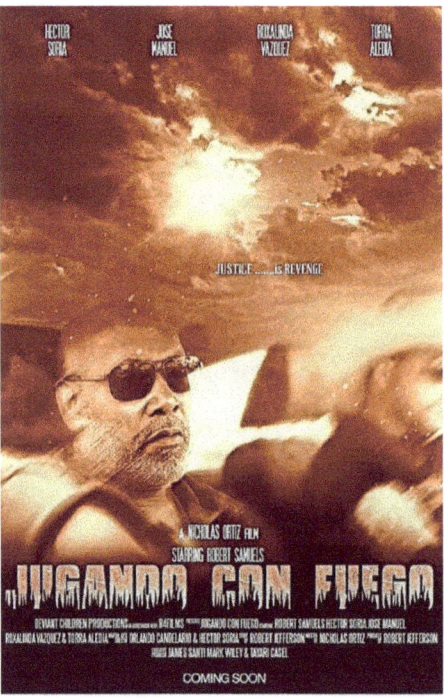

MMA, Judo, bladed weapons, and gun-fu, with a brief gore scene; that puts the icing on the cake. The fight scenes are well choreographed with sharp camera angles showing the true potential of the film and its creators.

SP: How did this film come about and how did you get involved?

RS: My partner Robert Jefferson and I discussed the idea of doing a film in the vein of Denzel Washington's "Man on Fire". We talked about some ideas but it wasn't until we spoke to Orlando Candelario, who has worked with us many times. Orlando recommended we should link up with Nicholas Ortiz who he's worked with on many occasions, to see if this is something we could all join forces on.

I had seen Nick's previous film "Black Beauty" and I was very impressed with his style as a director. We had many meetings and Nick liked our concept. He asked if he could write the script and we said yes! There was a certain sense of trust that had to be given for this work. The final script blew us away. We all signed off and pre-production began.

The goal was to tell a story and present a unique visual style to wow the audience. This would be my first film as a lead actor and not a co-star. I wanted to show that I could carry a film as the lead protagonist....but I'll let the audience make that decision.

SP: The film has a lot of good reviews, and nominations for awards and the momentum is building; what are the plans for the future? Are there plans for this film to be revisited or is there something new on the cards?

RS: We were blown away at the responses from the festivals across the world. Short films don't usually make a tremendous amount of noise because of the nature of how those films are marketed and it's a difficult sell with the big distributors. However, we do plan to release the film sometime in May 2022 for audiences around the world.

It will be released with a bonus short called "Behind the Bullets". We want the audience to not only see the film but to experience the adventure of shooting an international production.

In addition, we will use the film to show potential investors that the big screen version of this film is a great addition to the slate of films coming in the next year; with an original concept, great action, and characters the audience can root for.

SP: The fight scenes seem to have an ode to different eras and disciplines of martial arts. The first fight is quite traditional, then to the more modern bathroom scene, how was it training with the Action Director, Orlando Candelario? Did you have much influence on the fight sequences?

RS: Yeah we didn't want to create Hong Kong-style action per-se. We wanted to make sure the action complements the story. So Orlando Candelario & Hector Soria took their time to make sure each action sequence had its own narrative feel.

We didn't have a ton of time to preview the action so we made sure to map out each action scene to compliment the story. Most of the heavy action builds in the third act to make sure the audience takes a rollercoaster ride to the end of the film.

There is an action team, run by Angel Brophy in Tijuana, called "B-Squad Action Design". Angel and his team came on board to help us with creating the action. All the action motifs have their own feel; nothing is the same from scene to scene.

SP: The "making of" documentary is very well edited and reminiscent of 90's street films with the fisheye lens, time-lapse, decent music, etc. which I love; was the film as easy to make as it seems, or did you face any issues?

RS: Yeah so the plan was to create a special featurette to accompany the film as we realized that the film is just under a 40-minute run time but we also wanted to have a bonus for the audiences to show how this journey occurred. We plan on releasing the "Behind the Bullets" special along with the film, which will give audiences around 75 minutes of content.

The film was easy to make because of the amount of time pre-production took. We spent five months, planning, planning, and planning! We had to because we were not only shooting in the United States but in Mexico as well.

Special thanks to the Santi Brothers and our U.S-based Executive Producers Mark Wiley & Tayari Casel who supported us at every turn in the production.

SP: What are your best memories about making this film?

RS: For me, the best moment about this film was having a team and a director that understands how to create visual images to capture the audience's attention. The people of Tijuana, Mexicans are simply amazing people. The love and support we experienced cannot be put into words. Plus the local producers in Mexico made sure we had everything to pull off the film. We are forever grateful.

Shadow Fist

Shadow Fist (2020) is a Short with a running of approximately seven minutes. It is set in an alternative reality where we are introduced to two fighters in CGI. This morphs into live-action where it starts

with two masters, Dragon Chan (Robert Samuels) and Tiger Lu (Andre Duza) facing off within a forest.
The story progresses throughout the fight and without words, the relationship between the two is told through facial expressions and movements. The fight contains a myriad of forms that are impressive to even the most seasoned Fu fan.

Iron Bridge Chan (Sharif Anael-Bey) appears from the undergrowth and attacks them. Hai and Lung, confused at first, realise they must team up if they have any chance to defeat Iron Bridge Chan; building up to a cliffhanger ending.

The short showcased sharp modern production with an ode to old skool kung fu films including the sound effects. The music is keeping in theme with old skool films and is reminiscent of Shaw Brothers soundtracks. It is clear why this short gained traction and people wanted to know about the backstory, what led the characters to this, and what happened next....

SP: How did Robert Jefferson and you originally come up with this concept and turn that concept into reality?

RS: We always like to challenge ourselves with original stories and concepts. So we thought about what the Martial Arts movie audiences appreciate would. We thought about the Golden Age of Hong Kong Cinema. So the idea was to create a loose story and concept Ala Shaw Brothers. My favourite Director was Lau Chia Liang. So for me, that was my motivation in how to design the action. Andre Duza who served as Assistant Action Coordinator also did extensive research on making sure we kept the Shaw Brothers signature style in all the action sequences.

SP: Forms such as Snake, Tiger, Hung Gar, Wing Chun, and more are   showcased; how much training do the actors do together to make the moves look so natural?

RS: So for this film the essence of the Martial Arts had to be rooted in the same formula as the old skool Shaw Brothers films. I designed the action along with Andre Duza; the rest of the Action team.

Sharif Anel Bey is a FuJow Pai Sifu, Andre and also is trained in Chinese Kung Fu. Of course, I trained with Sammo Hung for many years in Hong Kong the key was making sure all the actors had their own signature styles and making sure the action was an extension of their characters.

SP: The atmosphere, sound effects, music, and style of photography resonate with old school fans, were you guys surprised by the reaction and popularity of Shadow Fist?

RS: Absolutely we were surprised. We didn't realize that there was still an audience that liked and appreciated the old school style of action so much so that the fans wanted more.

While living with Sammo Hung he taught me that while creating films over the years the most important part of that process was the Character he said always create characters the audiences can live thru vicariously So when we were casting for Shadow Fist 1 we already had an idea of how we would portray the characters. In addition, we talked with Music Producer Reese Tanaka about creating the music and scoring the film.

He wanted to preserve the true essence of the early days yet give it that modern feel of today's hip-hop vibe. Sound effects as well he wanted that Shaw Brothers flavor to draw the audience to that era. I think it worked.

SP: How did the sequel, Shadow Fist 2: Axe Gang (2022), come from an idea to fruition?

RS: Well to be honest we kept getting feedback that they wanted to see more content. So Robert Jefferson and I decided to take the next Chapter to a different level. We thought about how we could take the story and move it forward. Both of us loved the Chow Sing Chi film Kung Fu Hustle; the Axe Gang scene was part of the inspiration. Robert Jefferson then began to pen the script once I read it and I knew it was exactly the right way to move the story forward.

SP: Shadow Fist introduces a concept that encapsulates modern martial art cinema balanced with the classic Chinese Kung Fu film era of the 1970s and 1980s. Shadow Fist 2: Axe Gang goes deeper and more brutal into the world of the Shadow Fist.

Shadow Fist 2: Axe Gang

After the popularity of Shadow Fist; Shadow Fist 2: Axe Gang went into production in 2021 and was released in 2022. This Kung Fu Noir film progresses the concept of the original short.

This tells the story of Master Lung Chan (Robert Samuels) seeking the scroll of the Shadow Fist technique to learn the ultimate fighting form. The Lung Chan orders his disciples Snake (Andre Duza), Tenga (Elise Greeve), Lion (Anthony H Blong), and Kitusune Ryu (Anthony Scanish) to obtain the scroll at any cost scroll which is held by Sun Chien (Marco Johnson).

This is a story of loyalty and betrayal as each fighter searches for the scroll, building to a climactic ending. Sun Chien faces several disciples to save the scroll from falling into Lung Chan's hands. Lung Chan leads his posse from the front and Robert Samuels showcases a multitude of martial arts from classic Chinese animal styles to hard-hitting self-defense techniques. Stay tuned until after the credits as Tayari Casel's character shines new light on the illusive scroll.

Shadow Fist 2: Axe Gang showcases a multitude of martial art styles and techniques. The first encounter, a fight between Sun Chien and Kitusune Ryu,

showcases Chinese vs. Japanese martial arts. This fight is highly skilled and has already been said to be reminiscent of Drunken Master and The Way of the Dragon.

Elise Greeve's performance as Tengu is outstanding from her first appearance which includes one of my favorite camera shots, to her kinetic and her powerful skills against Sun Chien.
Lion has extraordinary sequences against the enemy until his morals are tested by Snake. Snake is a pivotal character throughout the story but not quite the

protagonist. Andre Duxa's abilities and presence shine throughout and I believe this will not the last we hear from Andre.

I have been vocal about my support for R4 productions and their potential to achieve mainstream audiences which I stand by. To make it nowadays, you need more than just a good actor or director, you need the whole package.

Shadow Fist 2: Axe Gang showcases an atmospheric soundtrack throughout that creates tension and compliments the storyline. The fighting styles have an ode to old school forms and modern techniques; adding the cinematic, this is truly a treat for any fight fan, new or old.

SP: The fight sequences within this film are jaw-dropping; do you work with the other martial artists/ actors to choreograph the sequences or do you choreograph it all yourselves like in Jugando con Fuego?

RS: Well Jugando Con Fuego was Action directed by Hector Soria Orlando Candelario and B SQUAD Action for Shadow Fist 2: Axe Gang It was my Action Team that designed the action. Andre Duza who is the Senior Member of the Action Team served as Assistant Action Coordinator. We worked for months rehearsing and fine-tuning all the intricate Kung fu moves. Although the film is around 30 mins it took about a year to complete.

SP: How do you balance creating fighting scenes that appeal to mainstream audiences whilst also appealing old school fans and practitioners?

RS: That was the tricky part we didn't want to be clichéd and just repeat scenes from old movies. So we made sure that every action motif had its own signature moves designed with the actor in mind. it's making sure the actors have scenes that are unique to their performance. Giving it that old school fee but keeping certain modern sensibilities about the flow of the movements

SP: Were there any injuries on set?

RS: Absolutely every time we film there is always the potential for injuries. We all got hurt at one point or another nothing serious. It just goes with the territory. There are several shots in the film that impact were made; I decided to use those takes as it adds to the realism of the action.

SP: The story is also told through sound effects and music; which enhances the tension and emotions of the film. How did you create the music and sound effects to fit the film?

RS: Yes we wanted to make sure not only does the visual style move the story but the music was just as important. We talked with Award Winning Producer Reese Tanaka to see what his thoughts were. He decided to reach out to his contacts and brought other Producers on board. Kollectiv, Genosha Records, Weapon E.S.P. Ghost of the Machine, and Lo Gun. They even create a title Track for Shadow Fist 2. Tanaka wanted to make sure we keep it true to the theme of the movie yet he wanted to have a modern flavour to the overall feel of the film.

SP: Do have any stories about the making of Shadow Fist?

RS: Yes, so when we first attempted to do this project we knew there were two people the film would be dedicated to Lau Chia Liang and Fu Sheng. I wanted to get the blessing of each of their families before we even attempted So I asked Fu Sheng's family and Lau Chia Liangs heir and they both gave me their blessings to do the film dedication. That gave me so much more motivation to make sure I got it right. So a lot of the action scenes are designed with Lau Chia Liang in mind.

SP: The traction and fan base of Shadow Fist are evolving; are there any plans to continue this story?

RS: Well of course we want to do another one but it's up to the fans. We already know where to take the story to move it forward and we've been in talks with our potential lead. The third Chapter will have a female lead and will be filmed outside of the United States. Roxalinda Vazquez is fast becoming one of Mexico's biggest action stars everyone loved her performance in Jugando Con Fuego; Final Contact Zero so I feel this would be very interesting to change it up with a strong female lead.

SP: Do you have any other projects you are working on? If so, can you tell us about it?

RS: Yes, we are still in Production now for Blackout; the Series re-joins me with Director Nicholas Ortiz. Once again it is story-driven Action /Thriller starring Angel Brophy Roxalinda Vazquez, Miguel Alexandro Peralta. Look for that in the first quarter of 2023. Shadow Fist 2 Axe Gang will drop first on VIMEO On Demand sometime in October.

SP: The beauty of short films is it has given great directors a platform to showcase their talent and progress within the US film industry. It is rare to see productions of this quality and substance.

Thank you for taking the time to talk with us do you have any last comments?

RS: We want to thank everyone that helped us achieve this film. Special thanks to Simon Pritchard and Rick Baker and the entire staff at Eastern Heroes Magazine.

CARL SCOTT
THE MAN, THE MYTH THE LEGEND

Interview by Rick Baker

"I was in Enter the Dragon" but blink and you will miss me"

I was fortunate enough to track down Martial Artist and Grand Master Carl Scott, whom I had been a fan of due to his roles in a few of my favourite Movies. I will be meeting up with Carl when I attend the "Urban Action Showcase" being held in "Times Square" new York November 4th/5th and had decided to (along with the other guests) put him on the front cover and follow up with an interview allowing readers that are not so familiar with his work to discover the guy that had late night audiences cheering in the cinema as they watched him move like a panther demonstrating martial skills on an equal level to those that crossed his path. His film career was short but the impact he made still had people asking "what happened to Carl Scott" well he is alive and well and looking to make a comeback.

I dived straight in to get the facts from Carl.

RB: so Carl, you were obviously doing martial arts from a young age?

CS: yes sir! Well I actually started doing martial arts at the age of six.

RB this was before the Bruce Lee craze began?

CS: yes this is way before then, my uncle who was in the military started me of doing "SHOTOKAN KARATE" and I grew from Shotokan to "KEMPO KARATE" under the leadership of Steve Muhammad, and I did many, many years of training both in fighting and competition.

RB: when did you start in the film industry?

CS: Well, they need extra fighter at one of the Hollywood studios, and the way that I got started was that the director who was over from Hong Kong was in attendance, and he was

there because they were filming "Bruce Lee the man the Myth" and I was an extra on that movie, and when we had a break the director (See-Yuen Ng) came up to me and thanked me for what I was doing and I was kind of just nodding my head because I did not really understand a word he was saying (laughs). And one of the cast members was looking at me move around during the break with some of my martial art brothers and they actually wanted to challenge me just so they could work out with me.

RB: you must have been young at the time?

CS: yes, I was around 17 years old at the time.

RB: What was it like sparring with them?

CS: So I told them we can spar and move around, but do not hit me in the face! Let's just go easy. Well the first move the guy did on me, I swear he tried to take my head off!! So when I moved back from that I thought "OK" I told you not to aim for my face, so I turned it up a notch. And I believe at that moment that I did not have the kind of skills, but he was about to be surprised (smiles)

RB: I remember back in the day at late night screenings of Kung Fu movies that when the audience saw you on screen went crazy with the way you moved like a panther equally demonstrating skills of the same if not better on the big screen. Now your back ground was mainly karate which is quite a solid rigid style, and yet you moved with fluidity in the movies.

CS: Well, I was very limber back in those days, and I had the ability to adapt to whatever style was in front of me, I was like a big sponge when it came to picking up different styles and being around a lot of guys that did Kung Fu and this enabled me to pick up on a lot of their moves that I could incorporate into my system. When I finally got to Hong Kong I started training in Chinese boxing and leopard styles which also played into the movements I was doing.

RB: what made you go to Hong Kong?

CS: I was invited after they saw me at the Hollywood screening to come shoot my first film, well just for your interview I had a very small part in "Enter the Dragon" but because I was so small it's difficult to see me.

RB: stop right there! You was in "Enter the Dragon"

CS: yes! I had a very small part, I was right by the door when Jim Kelly comes into the karate school and he had come to see his brothers, which was Steve Muhammad at the "BKF". Now when they came to do the filming they wanted a lot of the taller guys at the front so they could be seen punching, so the camera pans across and it goes right over me.

RB: was you aware of who Bruce lee was at the time?

CS: Honestly, at the time I was not totally aware of whom Bruce lee was.

RB: it was "Enter the Dragon" that really opened Bruce up to the West, he had starred in the likes of the "Green Hornet" but for most that was not the beginning of becoming aware of how much this one guy would open up the world of Kung Fu and martial arts cinema.

CS: I actually enjoyed the "Green Hornet"

so much but I was oblivious to the fact that it was Bruce lee playing the part of Kato at that time.

RB: So you was in "Enter the Dragon" but never actually met the

great man himself because imagine if you had got a picture with him how that would take pride of place in the photo album.

CS: Well, before he passed away there had been "rumblings" that I might get a part with him in the next Warner Brothers produced movie but of course he sadly passed just after completing ETD.

RB: So you might have been the next Jim Kelly?

CS: Exactly, had I ever had the chance to star in a movie alongside Bruce this would definitely had propelled my movie career, I mean looked what it did for Jim and Chuck Norris and Bob wall.

RB: I know! I mean if you had met Bruce, or appeared in a movie with him, you could have live of those stories for the rest of your life.

CS: I know! and when I was in Hong Kong working for Eternal films some of the cast who I met took me around and showed me some of the places he trained, they took me to the hospital that Bruce was taken to when he passed away, and they told me the way I had fluid movements and that I would have been a good fit should I had be given opportunity to be in one of his movies, and I thought that was one hell of a compliment they paid me.

RB: When you saw Bruce in his movies, let's say after "Enter the Dragon" was released was he an influence on your fighting style?

CS: yes! Very much so, I love the way the camera caught him on films and the way he would strike a pose for the still photography pictures

RB: Bruce's face, had so many emotions, and remembers Bruce was a Child actor so he was used to playing to the camera.. So you have gone to Hong Kong that would have

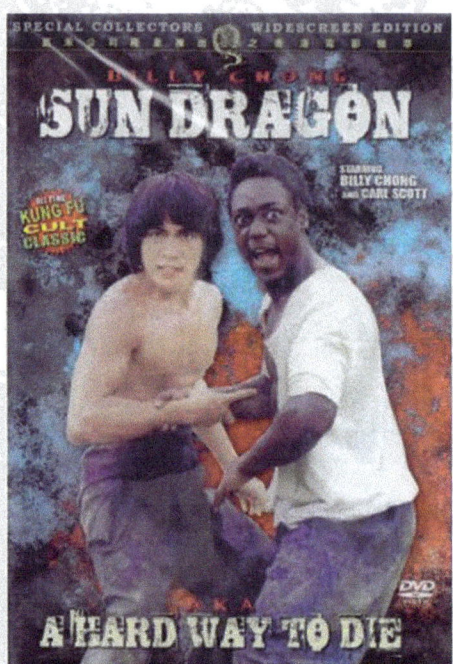

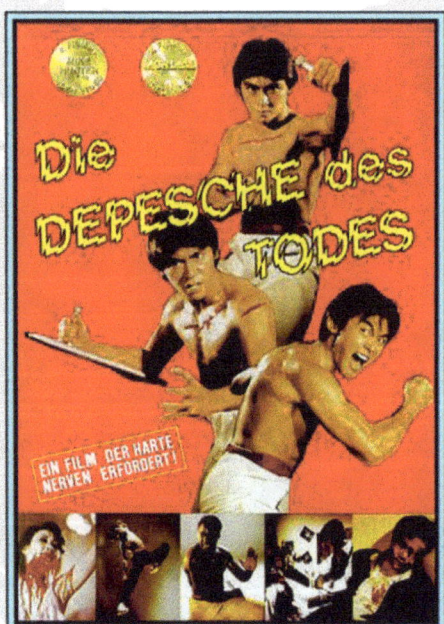

been for the Bruce Li film "Bruce Lee: The Man, the Myth (1976)"?

CS: yes it was.

RB: So how was it working alongside the legendary Bruce Li?

CS: He was really good, and he was a real cool guy. Bruce Li was real nice to me and whilst I was there in Hong Kong, he taught me a lot about film. Remember this was my first film so I had no prior experience in film.

RB: I guess back then when you were learning martial arts it probably had not crossed your mind that you wanted to become an actor/fighter in one of these Kung Fu movies.

CS: Well, unfortunately for me, I did not have that type of drive to become a Kung Fu movie star. Honestly at that time I was more interested in becoming a fighter, I really enjoyed fighting, sparring and competing that was my thing and at that age I did not have the fortitude to take my fighting skills and try to make it a career in the movies. Later on in life I looked back and realised I really did not have the opportunity like some of the guys there, but I knew that they did not have the fighting talent and abilities that I had.

RB: This is what was baffling to me, because your film career was quite short, and yet on screen you looked great and I think they missed a great marketing opportunity not casting you in other movies. The UK and I think I can speak for the USA audience they cheered when you were on screen back then it was unusual to see a Black guy fighting with as much grace as the Chinese guys that you were fighting. I think in total you appeared in four films, what happened?

CS: To be honest after those movies I was not given the opportunity.

RB: That is a shame because you look so good, I would have thought they would have been queuing up to put in their films, as like Jim Kelly I thought you was very marketable especially for the Western Audience.

CS: I know, people would come up to me and tell me how good I looked and were surprised that I was not in more films, they would say "Come on man, you looked great up there fighting and moving just like the Chinese guys"

RB: I remember back in the day at late night screenings, despite how good Billy Chong looked the talk after the film was about you. I mean back in the day they would send people to "Chungking Mansions" to scout out Westerners not just to be killed or thrown out of windows, but it added a bit of International casting to the production value and would often help putting a Westerner on the poster so it seem crazy that they would not make more use of you.

CS: Well I wish they had of been knocking on my door and reaching out to me, because that would have changed everything for me. But I came home and settled down and I have been married almost forty years, and I have a wonderful family and I decided to settle in with family life with my wife and three children being a good father and grandfather now. You had to make choices, leave my lovely wife at home pregnant whilst I went off and made movies or stay at home, I decided to settle in to my family life and through doing that I have a wonderful family.

RB: I think the latter was the better choice, a lot of people who have pursued film careers have at the expense of their own personal life so I respect your decision. Can I ask who, how did you find working with Billy Chong?

CS: Well Eternal films brought us together and they wanted to do a set of dynamic films with us, but for whatever reason this did just not happen. I was told that we had about three movies that they wanted us to do together and in the end we only made two which were "Sun Dragon" and "Kung Fu Executioners" and after that I never heard anything back from them.

RB: Billy back then was a star in Indonesia?

CS: Yes, he was a superstar in the soap operas in Indonesia, and I think after we finished are two movies he went back to resume his career in television.

RB: I felt that Billy did not have the longevity either, and he was great on screen and had a good look, I was a big fan but unlike Sammo and Jackie he sort of faded away after doing some great movies. I had heard he was difficult to work with; he did make a fleeting appearance in "Aces go Places 5) But I heard from a source working on the film that his role was cut down due to various reasons.

CS: well to me it was there loss, because if they had explored me more, I think they would have made a hell of a lot more money had they kept the partnership going between me and Billy.

RB: it's true, because I do not feel they realised how well these movies took off when they played the Chinatown cinemas and the fan base that you had created with your on screen fighting because those screenings were mainly attended by Black Audiences that cheered at those films so I think they missed out by not having you in more movies.

CS: Well I attended a movie screening here in the USA, and they asked me to come outside and sign some autographs. Now the audience had enjoyed the movie very much up until the point where they had a rope around my neck, and I was supposed to have been beaten up and then hung. And the audience took off; they hated that so much, so they sent me back to Hong Kong to re film that scene.

So they changed it so when they had the chain and rope around my neck and they showed me with my eyes open and that I had not died, so there are two versions of that movie out there. I think they protested with Eternal films to change the ending in Hong Kong so back I went and they changed it.

RB: Good! Can I just say one of the best opening scenes for me is the opening of "Kung Fu Executioners". It's the music drums beating and your using those nunchakus like Bruce Lee was that influenced by Bruce lee, because you looked like a natural, great opening.

CS: I could use many weapons and the Nunchakus and for me I found using them real easy to pick them up two sticks linked by chain and throw them around my body, and when people saw me use them they were blown away they were like "HOLY CRAP"

RB: I was not such a natural and ended up hitting my head and doing more damage to myself than whoever was attacking me, who suggested that you use them for that movie?

CS: Well they asked me what weapon could I use, and I replied "Whatever you want me to use" and they showed me the nunchakus and I said "Sure I can use them real easy" and once I started performing with them they just looked at me, so then they got me to use the staff and they said this gut can use almost anything so they wanted to work those into the movie.

RB: Again demonstrating so much talent and abilities with your fluid fighting and weapon skills they still did not pursue with you and offer you more movies to showcase your talent.

CS: I do not know, But working with Billy was great and who knows what might have happened had they continued with this partnership.

RB: Listen I could talk with you for another hour, but we will be meeting up at the "Urban Action Showcase" in New York this November so we can continue this and maybe do a part two.

CS: it was great talking to you Rick and I look forward to meeting you at the event and getting a copy of this magazine

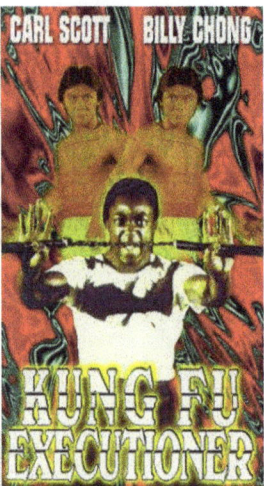

RB: For sure and I will make sure you sign a few issues for me (laughs) Take care till then and thank you for taking time out.

CS: thank you Ricky for giving me the exposure see you in New york

UASE 10
URBAN ACTION SHOWCASE & EXPO
LEGACY & LINEAGE

Demetrius Angelo is the founder and Exective Producer of The Urban Action Showcase and Expo (UASE). The UASE is the premier Action entertainment and Pop Culture platform celebrating diversity and

inclusion, honoring the past, present and future multicultural achievements within the blockbuster Action genre (Action, Adventure, Fantasy, Action Horror, Martial Arts, Sci-Fi, Superhero and Supernatural).

Since our inception, the UASE has become a key marketer in the dynamic production and promotion of diverse heroic content, by offering both fan and professional experiences. Our UASIAFF features the exclusive WarnerMedia Action Short Film Competition (formally Cinemax). Winners and Official Selections have gone on to obtain distributon with Cinemax, Amazon Prime, Tubi, and many others.

The UASE endeavors to Recognize, Promote, Facilitate and Encourage Filmmakers, Content Creators, Actors, Stunt Performers and industry professionals in the genre of Heroes.

The UASE recognizes creative expression by honoring excellence in various aspects of film making, acting and content creation through the Urban Action Showcase International Action Film Festival which features the WarnerMedia Action Short Film Competition.

The UASE promotes content creators through various media outlets, facilitate distribution opportunities and encourage new interests through the building of strong networking communities, panels, workshops and key sponsorship participation. The UASE inevitably inspires multicultural interest in the art of action film making, acting, production and content creation through the protocols of Information, Education, Facilitation and Exposure. The UASE fulfills its mandates through its Urban Action Showcase International Action Film Festival, Expo and Awards platforms.

UASE 2022 celebrates 10 Years of Legends and Legacy and we would like to acknowledge the many Action Fans, Sponsors, Icons, Directors, Filmmakers,Stunt Coordinators and Performers who have honored us with their presence through out our journey. Thank you for being a part of the Action!

UASE Alumni Honorees
Fred The Hammer Williamson (That Man Bolt, Three The Hard Way)
Grandmaster Ron Van Clief The Black Dragon (Return of the Black Dragon)
Taimak The Last Dragon (The Last

Dragon)
Kelly Hu (Martial Law, Lady Death Strike, China White)
Michael Jai White The Black Dragon (Spawn, Bronze Tiger, Blood and Bone, Black Dynamite)

Vincent Lyn (Operation Condor, Tiger Cage)
Robert Samuels (Don't Give a Damn, Gambling Ghost, Made in Chinatown)
Michael Woods (Tiger Cage 1 & 2, Blade 2)
Carl Scott (Soul Brothers of Kung Fu, Sun Dragon)
Mika Hijii (Ninja, Ninja 2: Shadow of a Tear)
Director Isaac Florentine (WMAC Master, Power Rangers, Undisputed 2 & 3)
Cynthia Lady Dragon Rothrock (Lady Dragon 1 & 2, China O'Brien, Yes Madam!)
Don The Dragon Wilson (Black Belt, Blood Fist, Ring of Fire)
Producer/Director Warrington Hudlin (House Party, Boomerang, Cosmic Slop)
Writer/Director Ben Ramsey (Blood and Bone, Dragon Ball Evolution, The Big Hit)
Brett Chan (Warrior, Kung Fu, Halo)
Andy Cheng (Shang Chi, Rush Hour 1 & 2)
Billy Blanks (Showdown, Talons of the Eagle, TC 2000)
Lu Feng (Five Deadly Venoms, Invincible Shaolin, The Flag of Iron)
Vlad Rimburg (Sultan, Inhumans)
Emmanuel Manzanares (Iron Fist, Bloodshot)
Dan Rizzuto (Wu Assassins, Van Helsing)
Ella-Rae Smith (Into The Badlands)
Ernie Reyes Jr. (Red Sonja, The Rundown, Teenage Mutan Ninja Turtles 2)
Cary-Hiroyuki Tagawa (Mortal Kombat, Tekken, 47 Ronin)
Keith Hirabayashi Cooke (Moartal Kombat, Mortal Kombat Annihilation)
James Lew (Big Trouble in Little China, Luke Cage)
Art Camacho (Half Past Dead 1 & 2, The Camacho Experiment)
Sherman Augustus (Into The Badlands)
JuJu Chan Szeto (Wu Assassins, CTHD: Sword of Destiny)

Marrese Crump (The Protector 2, Welcome to Sudden Death)
Javicia Leslie (Batwoman)
Nafessa Williams (Black Lightning)
Joivan Wade (Doom Patrol)
David Harewood (Supergirl, The Flash)
Anjelika Washington (Stargirl)
Damaris Lewis (Titans)
Mario Van Peebles (Posse, New Jack City)
Antonio Fargas (Foxy Brown, Shaft)
Gloria Hendry (Black Belt Jones, James Bond Live and Let Die)
Keith David (Pitch Black, Spawn Animated Series)
Jose Hernandez Jr (Oz, Gotham)
Kevin "Dotcom" Brown (30 Rock)
TJ Storm (Punisher: War Zone, Black Cobra, The Martial Arts Kid)
Michael Chin (The Last Dragon, John Wick 3)
Henry Yuk (The Last Dragon, Iron Fist, Warrior)
Christopher Murney (The Last Dragon)
Faith Prince (The Last Dragon)
Mike Starr (The Last Dragon)
Glen Eaton (The Last Dragon)
Kirk Taylor (The Last Dragon)
Janet Bloem (The Last Dragon)
Lisa Dalton (The Last Dragon)
Clayton Prince (Black Ninja)
Alyma Dorsey (Titans, The Matrix Resurrections, Star Trek: Picard)
R Marcos Taylor (Straight Outta Compton, Baby Driver, Luke Cage)
Lia Chang (The Last Dragon, Big Trouble in Little China)
Peter Kwong (Big Trouble in Little China)
Willie Bam Johnson (WMAC Masters)
Herb Perez (WMAC Masters)
Erik Betts (WMAC Masters)
Hakim The Machine Alston (WMAC Masters, Mortal Kombat)
Christine Bannon Rodriguez (WMAC Masters, Batman & Robin)

Jamie Webster (WMAC Masters)
Chris Casamassa (Mortal Kombat, WMAC Masters)
Janeshia Adams - Ginyard (Black Panther, The Falcon and the Winter Soldier)
Celia Au (Wu Assassins)
Cheryl Lewis (Luke Cage, The Gray Man)
Amy Johnston (Lady Bloodfight, Accident Man)
Sarah Chang (Accident Man 2, Blood Hunters)
Mayling Ng (The Suicide Squad, Lady Bloodfight)
Cung Le (Into The Badlands)
Perry Yung (Warrior)
Stu Bennett aka Wade Barrett (WWE, I Am Vengeance)
Marija Abney (Black Panther)
Jénel Stevens (Black Panther, Avengers: Infinity War)
Guy Stevens (The Warriors)
David Harris (The Warriors)
Dorsey Wright (The Warriors)

GAME OF DEATH REDUX 2.0

WORLD PREMIER
Screening and panel Q&A
Urban Action Showcase November 5th 2022
By Rick Baker

As I write this I am preparing to fly out to New York to attend the World Premiere of Alan Canvans magnum opus (Final Edit) of the long awaited "Game of Death Redux 2. After the screening I will be joined by Filmmaker Alan Canvan and Ric Meyers Writer, Critic and Media consultant to discuss and field questions in a Q&A. I would like to reprint my personal review of "G.O.D Redux 2.0" That was printed in my Bruce Lee "Game of Death Redux 2.0 publication" that came out earlier this year, to share my thoughts on this stunning effort from Alan.

I have always possessed an appreciation of Bruce Lee's unfinished Game of Death, dating back to my first viewing in 1978, when UK audiences were 'treated' to the most stripped-down version possible, thanks to the head of the BBFC, James Ferman, taking issue with the nunchaku scenes. Even though the worldwide release reinstated those drastic cuts that we suffered, there was still a great deal of footage that was omitted.

In more recent years, the internet has proven to be a fruitful source for allowing the masses to see the missing scenes discovered by Bey Logan when he worked for Media Asia. Various fan edits have emerged, providing – in their view – a more 'complete' version of Lee's opus. One such edit came to my attention in 2019. I was having a discussion with my old friend, Alan Canvan. He informed me that he had put together his own version of the film, called Game of Death Redux. I was incredibly excited to see his vision. I asked him if he would like the opportunity to exclusively screen his version to an audience at the Kung Fu Café in Stratford, London. He kindly agreed, and I was very excited to see his interpretation. Our optimism was justified - the audience, including myself, were very impressed with Alan's version. The cuts were excellent, and the edits provided a very fluid viewing experience. We even set up a video link at the end of the showing, so that the audience could ask Alan questions about his edit. I later discovered that the version we showed was actually a working print.

Such was its positive reception, that it was included as an extra on the Bruce Lee Criterion boxset, although Alan has since confirmed that the version presented in Stratford was slightly longer. Let us jump forward to 2022. Once again, I was talking to Alan about his latest edit of the movie – Redux 2.0. When I first read about his updated version, I was intrigued. I was very keen to get back in touch with him, to glean more information about the changes he had made to enhance the film. I was very fortunate that Alan took the time to bring to my notice many facets and details about Game of Death to which I previously haven't paid a great deal of attention. This has provided me with a deeper level of understanding, and made my viewing a much more complete experience. It has piqued my interest to ascend another floor of the pagoda. I have been fortunate over the years to spend time with many people who possess an excellent knowledge of Bruce Lee. The depth of their expertise, and their ability to discuss and debate every aspect of his films, has always resulted in a superior viewing experience for me. Alan's expertise has enabled me to reassess the film, and enjoy Game of Death in the same manner.

To anyone reading, I say this: read the interview between myself and Alan before you watch the film. It will enrich your experience immeasurably. Clear your mind of the previous times you have watched the movie. In its place, you will notice the time, effort and passion that Alan has invested in converting this end-of-reel sequence into a more complete piece of work. Every frame has been meticulously pored over, considered, and utilised in the best possible way. His dedication and love for the movie has created a self-contained

31-minute epic, depicting Bruce Lee's art at its best.

After our initial conversations, the time finally came for the viewing. I was more excited than I thought I would be. I was eager, with the knowledge I had acquired, to see this film from a new perspective. From the opening narrative by Alan, to Bruce Lee ascending the stairs, to the finale with him descending the stairs, I was absolutely transfixed. I didn't want to miss a frame. I wanted to give Alan my honest opinion about his new edit, and how it compared to the 2019 version, so I made sure that I viewed the movie through the prism of my newly-gained knowledge.

In a nutshell, it is a triumph. He has beautifully executed the editing, which enables the sequences to segue more organically than ever before. The colours have been enhanced where possible. The dubbing is vastly improved, and the war cries, rather than being stripped from an existing Bruce film, have been re-dubbed to create a more authentic sound. There is a real sense of context evident in his cries. The music cues are utilised incredibly well. Alan has built tension and used the music for dramatic effect throughout. Every scene is enhanced by his use of the soundtrack. I don't know whether or not we lavish enough praise on John Barry, but we should. His title score is magnificent, and its potential is realised fully in Redux 2.0.

Alan has presented this film from the perspective of a filmmaker. The only person to do that previously was Robert Clouse in 1978. There is a vast difference between a fan edit than that of a film makers cut. Unlike traditional film editing, which is characterized by a new assemblage of original film or video content, fan editing is a form of recombinant filmmaking that reactivates existing arrangements of audio-visual material. A film maker's Cut is a version of a movie that tries to match the director's original vision. Since most film Makers/ directors aren't given "final cut" privileges, it is the studio that dictates the version that gets released. A Director's Cut is typically released after the film has had an initial theatrical run. This "director-approved" version is typically released in the home video market. For "Game of Death Redux.2.0" Alan has approached this both as a film maker/and Director, to create a

coherent self-contained short movie in its best possible form creating masterpiece of art-house cinema. Let's be realistic! No other Bruce Lee film has showcased him depicting his art, his acting and his directing, and not forgetting the way he frames a movie like we witness in G.O.D Redux.20. This has only been achieved now by the aesthetic eye and dedication of Alan.

This is in laymen's terms, means we get, as the viewer, almost 30 minutes of Continuous Bruce Lee demonstrating his art over three levels without very little interruption when engaging each challenge. In conversation with Alan we chatted about the end scene, were Bruce is strangling Kareem, and the way the Camera glides from Bruce's face through the sofa panel to Kareems hand. This shot alone is worthy of cinematic recognition, that would be duly noted by any cinema buff.

In Summery this is not Alan offering up what he believes to be Bruce Lee's vision. No! This is Alan taking the ingredients of what is available, and like a Michelin Chef turning it into visual experience, by plating up a magnificent effort, combining music and the on screen charisma of Bruce Lee and making it a much more palatable experience for the viewer.

I can only stress that if you read and digest the interview between me and Alan, it is to be hoped that some (not all) will appreciate this new viewing experience with out fast forwarding in search of some new footage. And the next generation of Bruce Lee fans will view this first and not be mind cluttered with what has gone before.

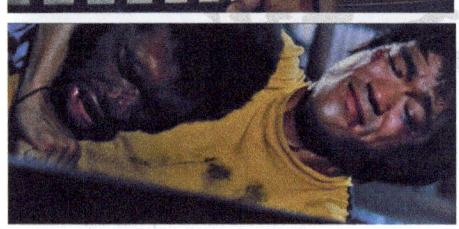

WIRELESS KUNG FU

By Alan Donkin
& Daniel Iarriccio

I have to be honest. I hadn't even heard of a radio spot until Daniel Iarriccio asked me if I'd write an article about them with him. The moment he explained what they were, I realised that I do know what they are. Of course I do. We all do! But I had no idea that they were things to collect, and that people collect them. It's an extremely niche, yet fascinating, hobby. So, without any more waffle, I present our chat about them in full.

AD: What are radio spots?

DI: Radio spots are vinyl records that were distributed from the middle of the 1950s until the middle of the 1980s for the purposes of commercial advertising, and advertising music and movies. Movie radio spots were sent to American radio stations to promote films that were released in cinemas. Most of the time you can find them in 45 RPM. However, there have also been radio spots in 33 RPM, but it seems far less common for the genre that I collect (martial arts films). I have never seen radio spots on martial arts films in 33 RPM, so to my knowledge they might not even exist, but you never know! You should know that most are recorded on one side and the duration is relatively short - between 20 seconds and 1 minute. For the radio spots that I own, you can hear a voice that promotes the film with sounds extracted from the film. I want to clarify that these discs were pressed only to my knowledge for the American market. I will also make it clear that it is possible to find spot radios on reel-to-reel tapes, because I have some.

AD: How did you first hear about them?

DI: While surfing on eBay in 2009, I discovered the radio spot of Enter the Dragon (1973) for sale. The seller who owned this 45 RPM had recovered an old stock of radio spots from a New York radio station. Gradually, he sold other radio spots featuring Bruce Lee films. However, his catalogue wasn't limited to Bruce – he also offered other movies, such as Screaming Tiger (1972) starring Jimmy Wang Yu, and Bruceploitation classic Goodbye Bruce Lee (1975).

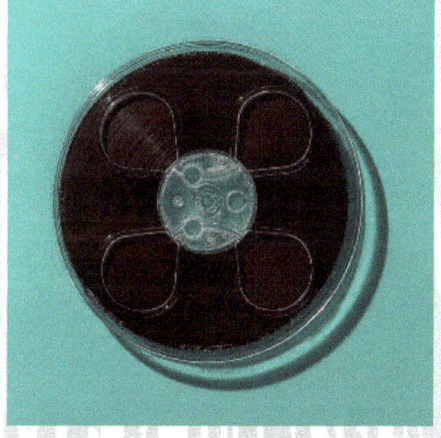

AD: Why did you start to collect them?

DI: I started collecting because I think these records are very important to preserve. They are part of the history of martial arts films in the United States. When I listen to a radio spot, although its duration is very short, it gives me the feeling of living in the era when martial arts films were playing in cinemas. Take, for example, the vinyl of Enter the Dragon that I have. I tell myself that this disc was listened to at the time by thousands of people, who heard it on their radios and were encouraged to go and see the film. The radio spot therefore contributed to the success of the film.

AD: Are they hard to find?
DI: Yes, some which are very rare. You should know that there are very few copies out there, because they were pressed in small quantities, and they were not intended for commercial purposes - they were only meant for American radio stations. The most frequent radio spot that I have seen is Enter the Dragon, because in my opinion, it has Bruce Lee in it. During the sorting out of material, it is the one that has been best preserved by certain

radio stations in the era, unlike other radio spots in which there was no Bruce Lee, which were destroyed more easily. But that remains a guess.

AD: How many do you have?

DI: I own about 40 or more, most of which I bought on eBay at auction, and a good half that I bought from a single collector. Speaking of which, for almost 10 years I pleaded with this great English collector to buy from his collection, because I had the ones he was missing and vice versa. After 10 long years he ended up selling them to me, and I still thank him today. He will surely recognise himself if he reads this article!

AD: Do you have a favourite?

DI: My favourite radio spot, and the rarest in my opinion, is The Chinese Profes-

sionals, also known as One Armed Boxer (1971). It is one of my favourite movies and it was important for me to have it in my collection. My second favourite, found recently, is the Shaw Brothers film Inframan (1975). It is not a martial arts film, but this radio spot is extremely rare.

AD: How do you play them?
DI: I am lucky to live in Switzerland, the country where the Thorens and Revox brands were born. I've always wanted to have a vintage setup. I listen to them on a Thorens 124 turntable, with a Revox amplifier and speakers. And, believe me, the sound is fabulous!

AD: Is there a large community of collectors?
DI: No, if we are only talking about radio spots concerning martial arts films in general. We number very few in the world. However, if we concentrate on the radio spots of Bruce Lee films, then the number of collectors becomes more significant.

AD: What is your 'Holy Grail' radio spot?
DI: My grail remains The Chinese Professionals, which I have found, but if I have to choose another to own, I would choose Five Fingers of Death (1972).

AD: What range of valuations do we see in the market?
DI: For most martial arts films released in radio spots that don't feature Bruce Lee, it is generally necessary to pay between 20 and 80 USD. But other radio spots which do feature Bruce Lee can sell for between 80 and 250 USD, because the community of collectors is larger. Finite resources shared amongst a wider pool drives prices up.

AD: Has the popularity of them increased at all since the resurgence of vinyl?

DI: No, radio spots have always been collected, even if the community of collectors remains small. I don't think the resurgence of vinyl has had an impact on the sales of radio spots, because it's advertising. Unlike vinyl, which is sold and sought after for its musical side.

AD: Are there one or more radio spots that you are looking to add to your collection?

DI: Yes! I recently missed a sale on eBay of a radio spot that I would have liked to have. It was Super Manchu (1973) with Cheng Yi. Another radio spot that I have discovered, but that I don't know if it exists on vinyl, is that of Kung Fu Mama (1973). My biggest regret is that in February I missed out on the Hammer of God (1970) radio spot. Trust me, it's very rare, and will be very hard to find again! It's always good to look for new missing pieces because it provides a challenge, and it would be boring to own everything. It is this permanent search that drives the collector.

ALAMO DRAFTHOUSE CINEMA
By Hector Martinez

I've always said to myself (and still continue to do so) that when I come into BIG money, I'm going to either build or restore an old movie theatre back to its original 1970's glory and screen nothing but 70's films with Kung Fu and Blaxploitation as front runners. I've always envisioned the theatre lobby decorated with original one sheet posters to the very films that brought me and my childhood friends countless hours of thrills and excitement while growing up in New York City, films like "Deep Thrust", "Duel of the Iron Fist", "Super Man Chu", "Seven Blows of the Dragon" "Fists of Fury" and dozens and dozens of others! As a child, my parents were very young (my mother had me at barely 16 years of age) and to pay the bills both my parents took on odd jobs to help make ends meet. While they were at work they would put me in the care of my favourite Aunt who for many reasons I have come to understand and accept that she is the one where I get my craziness and passion for what I do!

There was a movie theatre just a few blocks from where I lived called "The New Delancey" where they screened Spanish Horror and Wrestling films and my Aunt loved them! This is where we would spend countless afternoons staring at the giant screen with excitement and amazement. I'm talking about the late 1960's and early 70's. We later continued into the Kung Fu film explosion (including the Bruce Lee films) but of course as I grew older I went my own way but never stopped visiting this wonderful woman whom I shared such fun moments with. My Aunt has since passed away but what's fascinating is that the impact was so great that till this day I still have vivid dreams of the "New Delancey Theatre" I still see the box office, the Mexican Wrestling film "one sheets" out in the front advertising the theatre, the dark and gloomy lobby and the huge screen. It is because of this that I so passionately yearn to open up a theatre, it's the closest way to going back to that time and reliving that wonderful time and experience that every fan and collector dreams of.

Hector

Hector Martinez

Enter the year 2022 and The RZA, founder of "The Wu-Tang Clan" has teamed up with Tim League, Founder and Executive Chairman of the Alamo Drafthouse Theatre to bring us something very unique and similar to my dream: "The Flying Guillotine!" This outstanding area which is featured on the main entrance of the theatre consists of an impressive number of walls decorated with posters from just about every film that we watched during the 70's era, from Bruce Lee to Jackie Chan, Wang Yu to Ron Van Clief and Angela Mao to Cynthia Rothrock!

Hector Martinez

What almost knocked me off my feet (and had me holding on to my "neck") was the outstanding display they had in the main lobby featuring three different Flying Guillotines consisting of: the Guillotine to the first version from the 1975 Shaw Brothers classic "The Flying Guillotine" then the second Guillotine from the 1976 Wang Yu classic "The Master of the Flying Guillotine" and the third Guillotine from the 1977 Carter Wong classic "The Fatal Flying Guillotines" complete with decapitated heads and gore!

Hector

Hector Martinez

JACKIE CHAN
Project A
JACKIE CHAN
The PROTECTOR
COLOR
TWINKLE TWINKLE
LUCKY STARS
Samo Hung
JACKIE CHAN
SNAKE FIST FIGHTER
WAY
OF THE
CAT
JACKIE
CHAN
SNAKE IN THE EAGLE'S SHADOW

RESTROOMS
2
KNOCKABOUT
CONDORS
COMMANDO
DRAGON LUNG
JACKY CHEK
SCOPE COULEURS
TRIO
DYNAMITE

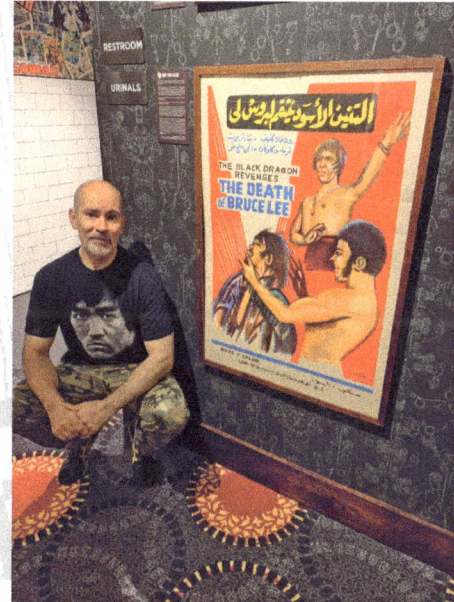

This phenomenal Museum/Gallery comes equipped with a Kung Fu themed Restaurant and Bar (with tables brilliantly decorated with an assorted array of 70's lobby cards) a gift shop offering limited apparel that feature images from the Flying Guillotine films, hats as well as original Shaw Brothers and independent film Kung Fu movie one sheets. The atmosphere is very hip as music from the Wu-Tang Clan plays continuously in the lobby reminding you that The RZA is responsible for this concept.

Even the restrooms are decorated with images of our favourite Kung Fu film Heroes. Visiting this theatre was such an inspiration helping me to strongly continue dreaming that my personal vision will someday materialize but at the same time giving respect to The RZA and Tim League for putting this wondrous together, it is the kind of magical place that once you visit you dare not leave, knowing that not one but THREE Flying Guillotines are on the premises waiting for it's next victim!
Hector
Hector Martinez
If in Staten Island come down and visit:

The Alamo Drafthouse Cinema 2636 Hylan Blvd Suite 230, Staten Island, NY 10306
Tele: 929-233-9660

Amy Johnston
The Blonde Fury

Interview by Rick Baker

A Little about Amy

Amy is an Actress, Stunt performer and Director, and a Rising star on the female movies.

My is known for many films including "Lady Bloodfight" "Deadpool" "Captain America: The Winter Soldier " and acting alongside Scott Adkins in "Accident Man" Her father is Dave Johnston, who was a former WKA professional kickboxing champion and was her first martial arts teacher. She is trained in Jiujitsu, Kenpo Karate, Silat, Escrima, Kung Fu, Kickboxing, Taekwando, Wushu, Wing Chun Kung Fu and Jeet Kune Do.

Amy was kind enough to do an interview with me. Both of us will be attending the "Urban Action Showcase" November 4th/5th so it was nice to have a catch up as I have put Amy on the front cover of this special "Urban Action Edition" alongside other guests attending this weekend spectacular.

RB. The first time I saw you were in the Movie "lady Bloodfight" and you looked pretty impressive.

AJ. Yes, it was a fun film with some good parts; thankfully we had Voltage Pictures who were on their producing who were an American team and because of their involvement I was happy to join the production.

RB. Back in the day the 80's 90's there was a big demand in Hong Kong for female action stars like Moon Lee, Yakuri Oshima, Michelle Yeoh, and then from the west we had Sofia Crawford and Cynthia Rothrock who found working on those early productions, stood them in good stead for when they started appearing in TV and movies back in the west.

AJ. Yes, there was some incredible talent back then.

RB. I am going to take a guess and say judging by the way you fight that you have been involved in Martial Arts for a long time.

AJ. Yes, I grew up studying Martial Arts, my father Dave Johnston was five times world kickboxing champion, and he owned a Martial Arts school. I was the first born so I grew up in a Martial Arts environment. And he would make it fun, we would create fight scenes and fall of things and of course we would watch action firms featuring a lot of the people that you have interviewed, so that was what I grew up on and it was always fun for me. I grew up as a Martial Artist and spent my life studying and so I always wanted to do something with it, and after watching all those films I thought I would like to see more females taking on these action roles, even though I had watch many great female stars in the movies I thought we still need more.

RB. You said you watched a lot of Martial Art film growing up, who where your influences apart from your father

AJ. Well, I loved Jackie Chan; I think he is one of the best physical actors out there! Also Cynthia Rothrock who was like this tough blonde girl was very inspirational. Michelle Yeoh was really my girl; I really liked her subtleties and her acting and the way she was feminine and strong at the same time.

RB. Totally agree, even when they

were fighting being thrown around but giving as good as they get back, they still retained a feminine but strong look

AJ. And it was still believable back then. Whereas today, in some of the bigger budget movies, with actresses trying to do their own stunts and They can be tiny and small and feminine, but you do not believe that they could do those moves Now with people like Cynthia and Michelle they looked good and you believed that they could do exactly what was happening on screen.

RB. Yes, with Cynthia, she had a good solid background in Martial Arts, with Michelle Yeoh and some of the other Asian actions stars, they would have to win a Beauty pageant with one of the TV companies. But what made them adapt on screen that they would have had a strong background in Ballet which allowed them to be flexible and easier to choreograph making their action scenes very believable.

AJ. Yes, I know that Michelle was a trained dancer, and I loved the way she moved on screen with grace, and I also grew up with dance I always wanted to be able to be able to bring the same performance when on screen.

RB. Back in those days the actors like Cynthia and Michelle, had to learn through "The Hard School of knocks" But by doing their own stunts in a movie, I felt it gave both the film and the actors more credibility when you watched them and it looks better.

AJ. I think so to, and I think it saves production time you can have more time in front of the camera, it's better for editing, as you do not have to cheat with angles like you have to do when your doubled having to hide their face.

RB. I totally agree, today with movies they can incorporate a lot of CGI and you can fake so much your eyes can be easily tricked into thinking what you are seeing is real.

AJ. I know, but I do think that people are tired of that now; I think "The Raid" hit it big because it looked it felt visceral and real, and I think people miss that, it's a more rounded fist to fist and I think the fans of action films miss that, they much more enjoy watching more grounded action, seeing the actors really going for it, and people are hungry for that. Right now they are trying to bring the female action back with actresses like Charlize Theron & Michelle Yeoh.

RB. There have been recently a lot of female style assassin movies that have come out in recent years. You

can see, that they train hard to bring realism to the role, and as you know it's a very physical demanding role, and I think what made the Hong Kong movies very appealing was that the action had a lot of realism actors and actresses risking their lives to film stunts, that in some cases made you wince, and your thinking how did they not end up in hospital falling from three canopies on to the roof of a car and get up to start fighting again!

AJ. Yes, you got to try to get the shot, and worry about the pain afterwards. Things are so different now; I have done a few documentaries because I have done a lot of stunt work and featured with other stunt women, discussing the history of stunts, and how things have changed so much. We have all these incredible pads and CGI and wires and all these safety precautions and insurance and so, it so much of a different environment today.

RB. It is, but not in Hong Kong, that safety can be all by the wayside on a small budget film, it's often about saving money, and let's us get the shot, even when Jackie was on the set of "Rush Hour" a massive production with the insurers making sure that it was all within the health and safety rules. Jackie would, revert back to Hong Kong shooting methods, jumping around on high level beams, with no harness turning Brett's hair white! Because that was how they would do it back in the day despite not having to put his life in danger it's just second nature to him.

AJ. That's crazy! I do love passion projects though, because a lot of people will come together, I have a lot of friends who grew up on Hong Kong action films, and that is how I started getting work making cool videos with my friends, and we would try to do the coolest stunts we could and save money by doing them ourselves.

RB. That's what we need, more passion projects! Even some of the older action stars from the 80's and 90's are still in good shape so your career is no longer over in your late to early forties if you take good care of yourself.

AJ. Sure you can see that in movies like "The Expendables"

RB. A lot of people that I have interviewed for the magazine, really had not considered becoming Action stars, but due to being in the right place at the right time, (back in the day) were spotted and offered roles which turned into careers. Did you plan to end up in movies or did you have other aspirations.

AJ. For me, it was absolutely my intention, because for one I grew up on those films, doing martial arts and doing a bunch of performance theatre and dance, and I loved performing. My brother and I would create all these fight scenes, recreate fight scenes, then we would edit them, and to be honest with you that is all I ever really wanted was to do stunts, act and create scenes. So by the time I got to 16/17 and my friends where going to collage I started to think that it might be a waste of time and I really do not have the money and the money I have I am going to go to L.A and I will try to network and try to learn and knowing full well I am going to be broke for a long time (laughs).

RB: Well, I admire that attitude, but was you not worried a pretty girl rolling up in L.A you could seem quite venerable and you do hear some horror stories and producers and directors trying to take advantage of you; it must have been hard! Forget about finding your way into the movie industry, but just trying to navigate your daily routine in a strange place.

AJ. Definitely, but to be honest, it was scarier for me not to try and fail and stay at home. So failing was much scarier than going and dealing with whatever obstacles came my way. So I may have been from a small town and I certainly found myself having to deal with lots of learning curves on having to stand up for myself, but I had to find that fine balance and figure out how to go forward, but it was really hard In the beginning.

RB. So how did you supplement your income whilst you were waiting for that big break?

AJ. Yes, for sure, I did a lot of extra work to learn how to be on camera, and in-between that I would mainly work in spas and being a receptionist, but it took maybe four years to find myself financially safe to not have to work those jobs, and able to support myself from my film work. I got my first big job as one of Scarlett Johansson stunt doubles in the movie "Black Widow" and I worked on "Captain America: The Winter Soldier" and from there I was finally able to take off and focus on my career.

RB: So your hard work paid off!

AJ. Yes, that is such a problem, and I cannot begin to tell you how many people that I respected told me that you cannot so both, as you will end up disrespecting both sides and you are not going to be taken seriously. But you know five years later and things are a little different now and people would say "Congrats Amy" you did it, maybe a little bit of a different to the ways others have tried, but well done! and I still try to do both ways today.

RB. So how did you transition to get the leading role in "Lady BloodFight"

AJ. So at the time I was doing "YouTube" Videos and I and a bunch of friends would come together and we called ourselves "Thousand Pounds Action Company" and we were actor's stunt people, creators and we all loved video games and Anime, and so we would create fight scenes, and the videos did well and I started getting work from that. Then I got an audition, were I am beating up a bunch of guys in a gym and from that I got an audition for "Lady Bloodfight" to read the script for the role which I got. it was around a year later that I headed to Hong Kong to start filming the role and then I actually tore my ACL (is damage to the anterior cruciate ligament) just before I started filming, which was very embarrassing, but thankfully they waited for me to heal.

RB. I thought you looked great in the movie and obviously was a great chance to highlight your acting and fighting skills.

AJ. Yes it was great fun and I learned a lot and the movie as a whole is a decent movie and some great people to work with including the director Chris Nahon, and I was very grateful that I was offered the role as it was a great experience.

RB. Did that help springboard your career for other projects.

AJ. Yes, right after that I did "Female Fight club" (2016) which was a decent movie had some good moments, and that was a local shoot in L.A with Dolph Lungren. Then I got to star alongside Scott Adkins in Accident man. I also did a bunch of pilots with some smaller roles. I was for a while worried that I might be getting stuck into a certain genre, and I decided to say NO! To a lot of things that I was offered, and that also meant I missed out on a lot of opportunities. But, eventually I realised this is my power, and so I continued to create and be content with whatever the end result was, but more importantly not to let go of how I got this far.

RB. Well, I would say it very gutsy in this industry to be selective with your work, than just take on anything that comes your way, as Like we said previously, you can end up being "pigeon holed" and that can prevent your career moving forward.

AJ. Yes, exactly and I try not to get "pigeon holed" But have decided to take what I get offered and use it to the best of my advantage, by manipulating it to make it a good move for my career.

RB. Well Amy, we could go on for a lot longer but I hope when we meet in New York we can catch up and re visit this interview and talk about your new projects that will have come your way. I truly believe that there are good things in store for you so let's keep this going in a further issue as I am sure the readers will enjoy hearing more about you as they all love female action stars and right now being one is a great time with all the female leads you see in new productions. So thank you so much.

AJ. Thank you Ricky, and look forward to seeing you at the "urban Action Showcase"

Vincent Lyn

MOVIE HERO TO REAL LIFE HERO

By Rick Baker

Vincent is no stranger to the pages of Eastern Heroes. I have interviewed him several times for this magazine and he also a personal friend.

Many of my readers will already know Vincent from his work on some of the classic Hong Kong action movies including The Blonde Fury, outlaw Brothers, Tiger cage, Robotrix and of course fighting with Jackie Chan in the wind tunnel in Operation Condor".

But just in case let's have a quick recap by highlighting his bio. Forever winning in Chinese is Yong Sheng. Vincent Lyn was born to a Chinese father and a British mother. His English name is Sir Vincent Raymond Percival Lyn. Vincent is the kind of individual whom you instinctively know when you meet him that he is someone worth finding out more about and the more you peel away layers of the onion, the more impressed you'll be. He speaks in a soft voice with remnants of a British accent. He was born in Yemen as his father was stationed there with the British Royal Air Force.

At two years old Vincent and his family moved to Ethiopia, Khartoum (Sudan), Algeria, Netherlands, then England. He immigrated to the United States at age 16 and then to Hong Kong after his university studies. Not coincidently, Vincent's multi-linguistic son, who is also a recent USA university graduate, now lives in Hong Kong. if you look up the definition of a Renaissance man, you may very well see a photo of Vincent, His talents, abilities, skills and interests are far-reaching and as diversified as anyone you'll ever meet. In the following paragraphs are a summary of a few of his many accomplishments as they are truly vast and impressive.

He is also Social Justice: Creative Director for African Views, an NGO charitable organization with the United Nations and whose mission includes: identifying

and bridging cultural gaps, facilitating improvement of social and economic ties and promoting global partnerships for the advancement in the humanities. Focusing on cultural sustainability and cultural harmony, their projects include: cultural exchange programs and panel discussions in the areas of health, education, environment and economy. In this role, Vincent has presented his "on the ground" observations and research to African Views. When people refer to "Don't just talk the talk but walk the walk". Vincent is the living example of this. He has witnessed first-hand atrocities, rapes, and murders of women and children, mass killings and ethnic cleansing. He has been shot at and come within seconds of having his own life taken at the hands of Sudanese Rebels. What would have stopped most people, inspired Vincent to work even harder for those in need.

I recently caught up with Vincent to not discuss his film career but to focus on the incredible Humanitarian work that he has been doing for "The United nations"

RB: I started by asking Vincent what aspirations he had at school, as looking at his career he has been an action star, a Grammy award winning pianist, you, have mastered the family style Ling Gar Kung Fu and done modelling what was your focus on back then.

VL: Well back then I was a huge fan of Jacques Cousteau and exploration was something that appealed to me, being an explorer seemed such a cool thing. But, once we immigrated to the U.S.A everything narrowed in the focus

on Martial Arts and Music became more my direction. The thing was after I graduated, I knew I did not want to teach music, and things happen in a roundabout way and film came before the music, it was later I signed with PolyGram and the plying at Carnegie Hall all came later.

RB: When you say film came first what do you mean?

VL: I am talking about "Tiger cage" that was what came first.

RB: well that is unusual, because when people are focusing on their martial arts or on their Music they do not usually veer of track because both of those subjects can be time consuming.

VL: Yes, but things sort of moved in a different way, but you know I look at many talented artists, actually one of my favourites was Dudley Moore, who was a great Jazz pianist, and he was incredible talented more than people realise, but despite that it never really took off. His comedic talent on TV and then moving on to Hollywood movies allowed him to go back and return back to his music with a higher profile.

RB: unlike you, he despite him not being very tall, he became an unlikely sex symbol, the complete oppressive to you tall, dark and handsome (laughs)

VL: (laughing)

RB: to be honest when you mage "Tiger Cage "Donnie was not a big star at the time so your first role was not going to be with big well known stars with the exception of the Director "Yuen Woo-Ping" who was a talent in the industry so it might have not worked out for you.

VL: True, I was about to head back after that.

RB: I mean how did you get that gig? Usually when they are looking for a Westerner to get killed of as a villain they just use to pop round to Chungking Mansions and ask you if you wanted to be in a movie that day, I am sure that was not the same for you! Or was it?

VL: I had a contact in New York who put me in touch with film companies in Hong Kong and one of them was D&B films. RB did you do that because you wanted to get into movies?

VL: Yes, that was part of it, and I had to take the step or jump and go to Hong Kong, and I think maybe back then a lot of people might not have done that.

RB: Let's be honest, back then if you was not boots on the ground in Hong Kong an E-mail or sending your CV would probably not got you any work, they were always looking for people who were in Hong Kong either on Holiday or back packing or studying not going to the expense of flying someone in unless that had some added value to the production.

VL: well that is what happens, when I visited these four companies one of them being "Golden Harvest" I met with Raymond Chow who advised me that if I was to hang around in Hong Kong for five or six months we can find you something, unfortunately I could not stay that long. Apart from "Golden Harvest" and "D&B" I also met with "Cinema City" and "Bo-Ho Films" g

RB: So let me jump forward to what you are doing now dedicating your time to doing more Humanitarian work.

VL: Well, I guess most people in the current climate would deem doing this dangerous work, and it's not like you get paid for it. This work for me came around in 2015, at the time I was doing close

protection work for this family that was building infrastructures in East and West Africa and at that time we were visiting shelters. Children were being rescued from child slavery and for me the look and what I saw in their eyes struck a chord with me and right from that moment I wanted to get involved. To be honest I did not know how I was going to do that, but I was meeting other humanitarian's, activists, and people from the United Nations and people from UNICEF I was talking to all these people from all these organisations. I decided to basically I took it up by myself to start visiting these counties.

RB: at your own expense?

VL: Yes, I travelled to under developed countries, Thailand visited refugee camps with the view to help the people.

RB: How do you get credibility when you're visiting these under developed countries? I mean you could be a bad guy masquerading as a good guy.

VL: Well that is true, but fortunately I never had that trouble. In the beginning stages I put myself in precarious situations.

RB: Well I guess there is no rule book when you embark on these journeys; I mean there seems to be as many people genuinely wanting to help as there are people trying to exploit the se vulnerable people.

VL: And that is what happens, I went Palestine, Lebanon and Iran, actually all over the bloody place and it was then I decided to start my own non-profit

donations of any sort, and to be honest in the beginning stages I got angry with my own family and friends. And I was relating this to the fact that they would think nothing of spending $5.00 on a coffee and a cake, and yet that same five bucks could feed a family for a week. But after a while you realise that there are many other organisations out there trying to raise money and that maybe people after a while think well charity should start at home.

RB: well, in the UK we are constantly bomb barded with commercials, adverts in newspapers, people in the street or someone knocking at your door so you can feel like you're just in a queue with your hand out.

VL: well it's not just that, a friend of mine made me look at it in a different perspective, and if I had not gotten into this work I would probably just been like all other people, and I would not have thought about it in the same way and it probably would not have resonated the same way as when you actually witness these terrible scenes with your own eyes. And of course one of the popular answers when looking for donations was people would say why on earth would you travel ten thousand miles around the other side of the world when we have are won problems here, And of course that is very true! But for me it did not start at home, it started around the other side of the globe and that is why in the beginning my focus was on Africa and then more so in the middle east.

RB: Do you feel now that sometimes

this might not be for me, the travelling away taking you away from your loved ones, and the dangers that are round every corner in these under developed countries?

VL: To be honest as of yet I have never felt that, and again to be brutally honest there has been a couple of times that I could have easily bought it and put me in therapy for a year or two. But! Even with that when I reflect and think should I give up, I mean I can still do it, but I do not have to be boots on the ground. And no matter how much you think you have prepared for this you really don't know what you're going to come up but you press on regardless.

RB: I know that we see so much violence in movies and on TV but when you see someone shot in real life it has a totally different impact on you mentally.

VL: Just recently when I was in London and we met up, I was staying with an old friend of mine, and whilst I was there another friend sent me a video that he had just took of what looked like cruise missiles coming over his head and exploding into some nearby buildings, and he called his son over who was sixteen, seventeen and like most teenagers his son was into all these video games, and his son is looking at this video and there is no reaction and it was as if he was just playing one of his video games and that through doing that he had almost been desensitise to what he was seeing. The reality was that just 20 minutes people had been killed.

RB: So you seeing atrocities when you are visiting these countries, has this desensitised you?

VL: Absolutely not at all, I think we as humans when it comes to mass suffering and maybe it's a self-preservation, we just tend to look away and would rather not deal with it.

RB: I guess that is what we are seeing now with the Ukraine situation we see it on the news but as the bombs are not dropping in our back garden we can distance ourselves from the reality of the devastation. It's just so easy to change the channel or not read the front page headlines.

VL: I guess we can deal with one person, maybe a family member or close friend or just one image, we can usually cope with that, but when we start talking about THOUSANDS! And mass graves of thousands those kinds of numbers do not compute to most humans and it's easier to just look away.
So for me it does not really desensitise me, if anything it makes me more sensitive to the situation.

RB: so are you still just doing this on your own or are you attached to any other organisations?

VL: well I thought about this putting my organisation under the same umbrella as the UN and other organisations but on

reflection I do not think it would make much difference, and I am glad that I did not I do have a UN jacket that I ware but for me I would rather not get in bed with others as even today I had a message from a colleague high lighting a scam so I would rather continue on the path that I am doing than risk getting involved in situations beyond my control, it's tough but I know what I do is all above board.

RB: So what is your end objective when you go in these missions?

VL: So, like when I just went to the Ukraine, I firstly deliver the essentials, even though they are not asking for these, they would rather have weapons, but by me delivering this myself I know they are going to the right people.

RB: this has been such a fascinating chat and I know we could do a whole magazine on this subject as it is so important, and I take my hat off to you, because with all your talents you could be living a much easier life I am sure the readers will find this article heartfelt and touching and if they need to know more you can find Vincent on "Face Book" **https://www.facebook.com/vincent.lyn.50** And if you want to hear him play as a pianist I could listen to him play all day, Then Vincent returns to Carnegie Hall on the second of December 2022 featuring Billboard #1 Hot Singles Sales R&B vocalist Melissa B.

Thank you again Vincent and see you in New York for the "Urban Action Showcase" November 4th & 5th.

VL: Thank you Rick.

FANATICAL DRAGON PRESENTS
5 FINGERS OF DISCS

Greetings friends, some HUGE Blu-ray releases either just out or coming very soon which are all fighting tooth and nail for your hard earned cash, join me once more as I dive in for a quick look at some of the most notable ones…

1) **Shawscope Volume 2**
   Arrow Films
   Region A+B
   Available Nov 21st (UK) Dec 6th (US)

Absolutely THE best release of the year this one. Arrow have somehow managed to build on their incredible Shawscope Volume One set from 2021 and deliver an even better follow up. The number of films included in the set has been increased to 14 (from last years 12) and presents an incredible selection of Shaw's real heavy hitting highlights. We see their focus on Chang Cheh and Lay Kar Leung continue with strong examples from both Directors filmographies.

From Lau Kar Leung we get all three of the movies in his incredible 36th Chamber of Shaolin trilogy starring the wonderful Gordon Liu / Lau Kar Fei as well as the incomparable Mad Monkey Kung Fu and My Young Auntie, the two films in his filmography which best showcase the talents of regular collaborators Hsiao Ho and Kara Hui. We also get Pop's first feature film shot entirely in mainland China, the 3rd instalment of Jet Li's Shaolin temple cycle, Martial Arts of Shaolin.

From Chang Cheh we get Venom Mob starring favourites The Kid With The Golden Arm and Invincible Shaolin as well as the Magnificent Ruffians and the ensemble picture the 10 Tigers of Kwantung. The set is rounded out by the insanely popular Boxer's Omen which sits alongside the incredibly underrated Wong Jing film, Mercenaries from HK starring Ti Lung, Wong Yue, Johnny Wang Lung Wei and Philip Ko. The Bare Footed Kid Johnnie To's remake of Disciples of Shaolin is also present here and the set is completed with Lo Mar's Five Superfighters.

For long time Shaw's fans, this offers a wonderful upgrade to older DVD and VHS copies with brand new restorations for most of the 14 films, including a beautiful 4K restoration of 36th Chamber of Shaolin which has to be seen to be believed, for new disciples at the Shaw Brothers temple, this set is another incredible selection of 'must sees'.

There are also hours and hours of special features pulled both from the Celestial archives and created specifically for the boxset which would take me pages to properly list in full.

Highlights include the next two parts of the excellent Cinema Hong Kong Documentary (Part one was included on Volume One) Citizen Shaw, a French TV feature from the 80's which runs for almost an hour long and offers a wonderful time capsule of the Studio and some of its productions during that time period. Commentaries are provided for about half the films on the set, and are extremely well researched and entertaining to listen to. Tony Rayns provides select scene commentaries for The 36th Chamber of Shaolin and My Young Auntie and there is a truly fantastic track on Mad Monkey Kung Fu hosted by fellow Eastern Heroes collaborators Frank Djeng and Michael Worth. Brandon Bentley records his first track for Arrow Video on 10 Tigers of Kwantung and delivers one of the best Shaw's commentaries I've heard anywhere.

For anyone interested in a real deep dive into Volume2, I'm creating individual reviews for every disc in the set over on my youtube channel, you can join me as I explore each and every movie, special feature and commentary track on the entire set over at:
www.youtube.com/thefanaticaldragon

If you can only afford one big blu-ray purchase this Xmas season, make it this one. It's expensive yes, but given how many films you are getting and now many hours of bonus features, it's actually a very good deal, working out at a little less than £10 a film. I cannot recommend it highly enough.

2) **Police Story Trilogy 4K**
   Eureka Entertainment
   Region Free (Most 4K titles are)

I'm quite sure that most of you reading this, just like me, have more copies of Police Story in their collection than any other HK movie, so for another PS boxset to come along and manage to make itself an essential purchase meant it would have to be something pretty damn special and somehow, against all the odds, Eureka have pulled it off. The 4K trilogy boxset pulls together all the best bit of the previous Eureka release of PS1 and 2 and adds in the long awaited UK debut on Blu-ray (and 4K in this instance) of Police Story 3 aka Supercop (A standalone Blu-ray release of PS3 has also been released with identical extras to the 4K disc included in this set, more on that release next issue) The new remasters of all three films into 4K is spectacular, I actually upgraded to a 4K player specifically just for this release, and it was well, well worth the upgrade. I've never seen the movies looking so damn good, with this much details and this much vibrance. Three of Jackie's absolute

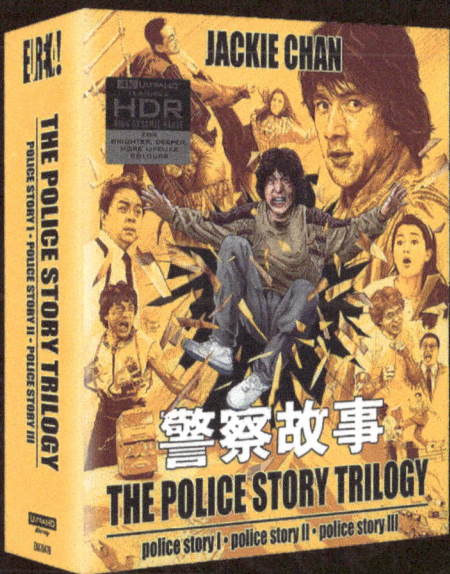

best, presented in their very best and accompanied by a raft of excellent and well balanced special features.

The set is a real triumph and for me, the best Boxset that Eureka have produced so far. The cover art on the set has been created by my Kung Fu Brother from another mother, the amazing Kung Fu Bob O'Brien who has created a stunning slice of box art pulling in elements from all three movies into one explosive and captivating piece. Two new commentaries for all three movies have been created, a track for each movie by Frank Djeng here joined across all three tracks by FJ Desanto and a second series of three tracks by the HK Dynamic Duo, Big Mike Leeder and Arne Venema. Arne has also taken to the streets of Hong Kong to create a video guide to various key locations used throughout the trilogy and also a separate and equally fascinating featurette looking at the ill fated but highly entertaining Jackie Chan Video Games. Both are excellent and I hope the first of many more extras that Eureka (and the other labels) will commission Arne to create, he's a thoroughly engaging and entertaining host and both videos are extremely well produced. We also get an all new interview with stunt co-ordinator and film historian John Kreng and a gorgeous bound book with writings by James Oliver alongside a raft of promotional stills and printed materials compiled into the 100 page book.

The vast bulk of the extras from the older Eureka PS1+2 boxset have also been ported over

and are rounded out with hours of archival interviews with Jackie Chan, Michelle Yeoh, Stanley Tong, Ken Lo and Benny Lai. The wonderful Jackie Chan Episode of Jonathan Ross's Son of the Incredibly Strange Film Show is also present here, itself a gateway for a great many of us here in the UK to finding JC for the first time. Add in the archive commentary fro PS2 by Miles Wood and Jude Power, trailers for all three movies and we get about as perfect a boxset as we could have hoped for to pull together the first three (and best) of the Police Story Movies. It's easily my most highly recommended 4K release of the year.

3) **The Iceman Cometh**
   Vinegar Syndrome
   Region A
   Available Now

The second big HK release from wonderful American Boutique label Vinegar Syndrome following on from their stunning release of Righting Wrongs. And again putting us in a strange position of having two different versions of the same movie coming out on different sides of the Atlantic, Vinegar Syndrome putting them out in the US and 88 Films bringing out their own deluxe versions in the UK. Different restorations, artwork and special features on each version may make the choice a tricky one for buyers with multi region Blu-ray players. But in this case, as with Righting Wrongs before it, Vinegar Syndrome have been the first out the gate and at the time of this issue going to print I'm still waiting to compare their releases against the UK counterparts.

Vinegar Syndrome have set the bar very, very high, both with their version of Righting Wrongs, and again with this release, the HK take on Highlander.. The wonderfully insane, The Iceman Cometh.

Starting out in the Ming Dynasty, with Yuen Biao's character Fong Sau Ching being tasked with bringing his brother Fung San (played with relish by Yuen Wah) to justice after Fung has been found to have killed several women. The two brothers end up frozen in ice thanks to a mystical device called the Wheel of Life and Death and find themselves being thawed out 300 years in the future and their battle resumes in 80's Hong Kong, with Yuen Biao initially becoming a reluctant man-servant to a very young and highly demanding Maggie Cheung whilst Yuen Wah works his way up through HK's underworld whilst resuming his old woman slaying antics once again.

It's up to Yuen Biao to continue his quest to bring the killer's reign to an end. A great mix of action and comedy make this, for me, the best movie director Clarence Fok made during this period and the package Vinegar Syndrome put together for the movie celebrates the film in style. We get some of the old Hong Kong Legends DVD interviews with Yuen Biao and Yuen Wah ported over to the Blu-ray disc, alongside an all new interview with the cinematographer of the film, Poon Hang Sang.

A commentary track has been provided by the wonderful Samm Deighan who delivers an extremely enthusiastic and informative track for the movie. We also get two separate cuts of the film. The shorter 115 Hong Kong cut as well as the longer 122min Mandarin edit of the film. Gorgeous cover art for the release has been crafted by Vinegar Syndrome regular Robert Sammelin.

Time will tell how the 88 film release stacks up against this VS edition when the 88 version releases in December of this year.

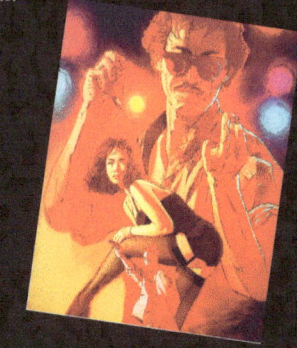

4) **Lady Assassin / Secret Service of the Imperial Court**
   What Price Honesty / Gang Master
   Spectrum Films
   Region B
   Available Now

I've previously spoken about the Shaw's releases being curated and put out by the fantastic French Label Spectrum Films in these pages before and my love for their Shaw's releases grows stronger and stronger with each new Bluray they put out. The next two double feature packs the label has brought out both showcase some lesser known but absolute gems from the Shaw's back Catalogue.

The first pack features The Lady Assassin and Secret Service of the Imperial Court both directed by Tony Lou Chun-Ku (Holy Flame of the Martial World, Bastard Swordsman), and the second pack puts together the woefully underrated What Price Honesty directed by Patrick Yuen Ho-Chuen alongside Gang Master directed by Tsui Siu Ming. All four were titles that often proved extremely hard (or expensive) to find on the old IVL DVD range and a proper upgrade to Blu-ray was long overdue and very, very welcome. All four of the restorations on show here look absolutely incredible.

The Lady Assassin is a fantastic slice of 80's era Wu Xia action, Secret Service of the Imperial Court and What Price Honesty both deal with more grounded Martial Arts against a backdrop of Police corruption, with the latter, What Price Honesty feeling like an especially brutal and honest take on political corruption which still has the power to resonate and in places shock today. It's a spellbinding movie and my favourite of the four new titles, with Lady Assassin coming in a close second. Gang Master is a more standard Shaw Brothers movie from this era, but still a very well executed example with a stellar cast (Chen Kwan Tai, Pai Piao, Ku Feng, Yuen Tak being standouts).

There are some extra features on the releases courtesy of the treasure trove archives of Frederic Ambroisine, however, these, like the film themselves do not come with English Subtitles, only French subs, but I implore you not to be put off picking these releases up.
My own schoolboy level french and my

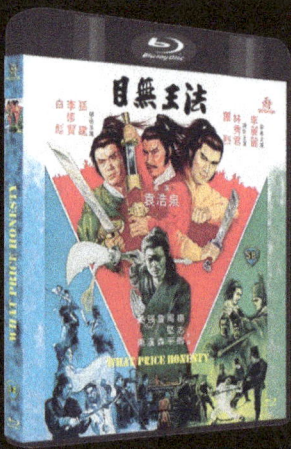

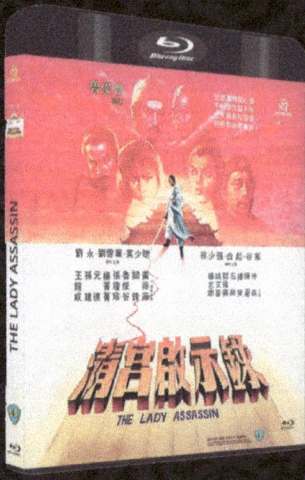

even more rudimentary Cantonese are vastly aided by watching the movies in Cantonese with French Subtitles. For this alone, these releases are a great learning aid to anyone studying Cantonese (or French) as the dialogue is fairly simple and moves quite slowly across all four titles. But all four titles, as with the four previously released in these double packs by Spectrum (Bastard Swordsman 1+2 and Holy Flame of the Martial World/Demon of The Lute) highlight some real Shaw Brothers cinematic treasures, I can't wait to see what others Shaw's titles Spectrum turn their attention to next!

Maybe in time we will see another label picking up these titles, but i wouldn't hold your breath for it! Spectrum are really diving into some truly wonderful titles are giving us glorious versions of them and that is absolutely worthy of celebration. The Two double packs both come with slipcovers featuring the original (and wonderful) HK poster art for one of the two titles on each set, the interior case has a reversible sleeve which showcases the art for the second feature.
ils sont magnifiques!

5) **On The Run**
   88 Films
   Region B
   Available Now

2022 really does seem to be the Year of Biao, we are getting so many fantastic releases of some of Yuen Biao's best movies coming out, and 88 films release of the Crime Thriller On The Run is way, way up there with the best of them.
Darker and less action focused that the mighty Righting Wrongs, On The Run gives Biao a chance to flex his acting muscles more than his acrobatic ones. The synopsis 88 films present for the movie states: 'In the aftermath of his wife's brutal murder, struggling cop Heung Ming (Yuen Biao) is forced to go into hiding after discovering corruption in the ranks. His only ally is a deadly assassin Chui (Pat Ha) as they each try to avoid arrest, and even death.'

This brand new 2k restoration of the 1988 movie looks fantastic and initially coming out in the form of one of 88's Deluxe Editions, is loaded with extras both in terms of printed materials (reproduction lobby cards, poster and book) as well as on disc extras. We get two feature length commentaries, one by the incredibly busy Frank Djeng, joined once more by FJ DeSanto and a separate track by the always engaging Podcast on Fire Network lads, Kenneth Brorsson and Phil Gillon. Both tracks are extremely informative and humorous, and its great to see 88 getting Kenneth and Phil back for another track again, their recent tracks for some of 88's Shaw's releases were also excellent. We also get all new interviews with director Alfred Cheung and the film historian David West and an alternate ending for the movie.

Cover Art is provided once more by the incredible Kung Fu Bob O'Brien who has created a Neon soaked tribute to the movie which adorns the cover and comes on one side of the included double sided poster. All in all, it's a really wonderful addition to 88's ongoing Deluxe Edition series and will be followed up with similar editions for Righting Wrongs and The Iceman Cometh along with 4K Deluxe Editions of Dragons Forever and Supercop (US only) all due out later in the year.

There are countless other Blu-ray and WK releases of HK and Asian titles coming thick and fast from the boutique labels both here, in the US and from elsewhere in the world. I can only ever cover a small selection here each issue, for more up to date information and for more in depth reviews and previews, please find me on Youtube where i upload videos regularly.

Written by Johnny 'The Fanatical Dragon' Burnett

www.youtube.com/thefanaticaldragon

Special Thanks to

Without valuable contributions "Eastern Heroes Magazine" would not have the informative information that we use to compile and make this great read.

Crike99Art cover design
Tim Hollingsworth: Designer
Simon Pritchard (UK)
Dean Meadows (UK)
Alan Donkin (UK)
Ron Ivey (UK)
Aiodhan M Cochrane (UK)
Shazad Asghar (UK)
Martin Sanderson (UK)
Micheal Nesbitt (UK)
Dave Cater (UK)
Thorsten Boose (Germany)
Jason McNeil (USA)
Hector Martinez (USA)
Demetrius Angelo (USA)

Special Thanks

Robert Samuels (USA)
Carl Scott (USA)
Amy Johnston (USA)
Ron van Williams (USA)
Vincent Lyn (USA)

www.ingramcontent.com/pod-product-compliance
Lightning Source LLC
Chambersburg PA
CBHW051324110526
44590CB00031B/4456